Animals Have Rights, Too

I am in favor of animal rights as well as human rights. That is the way of a whole human being.—Abraham Lincoln. Photo by M. W. Fox.

Michael W. Fox

ANIMALS Have Rights, Too

CONTINUUM · NEW YORK

1991

The Continuum Publishing Company
370 Lexington Avenue, New York, NY 10017

Printed in the United States of America

Library of Congress Cataloging-in-Publication Data

Fox, Michael W., 1937–
Animals have rights, too / Michael W. Fox.
p. cm.
Includes bibliographical references.
ISBN 0–8264–0523–1
1. Animal rights. I. Title.
HV4708.F718 1990
179′.3—dc20 90–41476
CIP

For Michael, Camilla, and Mara

Contents

Acknowledgments

I want to thank Professor Bernard Rollin, Department of Philosophy, Colorado State University, Fort Collins, and Ms. Iris Rainone, Stone Ridge School, Washington, DC, for their helpful criticisms and constructive input in the preparation of this book. Thanks also to Continuum's associate editor, Kyle Miller, and copy-editor, Deborah Cooperman, whose combined skills have really improved the quality and clarity of this book. I am also grateful for the resources of The Humane Society of the United States, and the inspiration provided by children of all ages who have helped me clarify and expand my vision of animal rights and human obligations. Without the insights and 'lessons' from the many animals, wild and tame, whom I have known and studied from early childhood, and the support and encouragement of my parents, this book would never have been conceived. To them especially, I owe my respect, gratitude, and affection.

Introduction

▪ For Parents and Teachers

Young children are extremely sensitive and impressionable, especially with regard to animals. They have a natural affinity for them and a curiosity which should be carefully nurtured. With the right guidance and encouragement by parents and teachers, a child can learn to appreciate and understand animals, to treat them with compassion and to respect their rights. In a purely utilitarian sense, animals can provide valuable learning experiences that will help a child mature into a more responsible and caring adult. In other words, teaching kindness toward animals can indirectly benefit society because humane attitudes affect our relationships with both animals and people.

A child who is encouraged to develop an awareness of the rights of animals will become less self-centered and at the same time will have a much healthier, and more sensitive and compassionate regard for others.

The question of animal rights has been ignored in our culture for too long. We owe it to them, as we do to our children, to foster concern for the rights of animals; to put an end to thoughtless abuses, exploitation, and insensitivity towards our animal kin that are so widespread today.

This book will make children think, feel, and see with greater intensity and clarity, just where we fit in relation to the rest of the animal kingdom, and what our responsibilities and obligations are.

▪ For Children (including teenagers)

This book is about the rights of animals and the wrongs that people do to them when they don't know anything about animal rights. I wrote this book because I am sad and angry about how people treat animals. People have an obligation to be kind to animals but often they forget or are ignorant about the fact that animals can suffer. Some people are simply indifferent. They don't seem to care at all. I often wonder what they learned about animals when they were young. If they had learned something about animal rights, they would be kinder and more considerate toward animals. This book is a chance to learn why people must be kind to animals, what rights animals should have, and how we can all help them.

The secret formula is really quite simple. All that has to be done is to get everyone to accept that animals have certain rights and that it is wrong for humans not to respect and uphold those rights. In some parts of the book I will ask various questions in order to make you think. A Greek philosopher named Socrates used this method a long time ago. When you really start to think deeply and to concentrate for a while you really do begin to feel and see things better. It is difficult, for example, to try to figure out just why people don't always respect and defend the rights of animals. And when we can think out all the reasons why, we will find many solutions to help animals.

I will give you lots of reasons why animals have various rights, such as the right to be treated humanely. When you know all about these rights, tell your friends and do your best to live up to those rights yourself. You will then be helping all animals, and you will be their friend and spokesperson as well.

CHAPTER 1

Why Rights for Animals?

Concern for animal rights is something relatively new. Up until quite recently, animals have been more or less taken for granted, but since they can't speak for themselves, we, as their masters, guardians, or protectors, must speak for them and defend their rights. It is because we use animals in different ways—for food, companionship, to help us find cures for disease, and so on—that we have certain responsibilities and obligations toward them. We, the most powerful animals on earth, have a moral obligation to protect and enforce their rights.

You and I have all kinds of rights. They came into being to protect our interests and are part of the law and of society's rules of conduct.

Grown-ups have a right to be respected by children when they wish for a little privacy or peace and quiet for a while. But for grown-ups to always demand that children be quiet and not bother them is a violation of a child's right to be a child. Remember, there is a difference between legal and moral rights. There are specific laws to protect certain human rights, such as the right not to be robbed or deliberately hurt by someone. The Constitution of the United States spells out a number of important human rights, which are upheld by the law. The right to freedom of speech is a very important one. There is a new law that gives anyone, no matter what race they belong to, the right to have a fair and equal opportunity to apply for and be hired for a job. These are all moral rights which have been written down and put into law so that they are legal rights. It's illegal therefore for someone to be denied their right to freedom of speech (to express their views publicly) or to have a fair chance to get a job. Handicapped children have a right, which is backed by a special law for them, to receive special education.

While there are laws that say you shouldn't steal from someone or hurt them physically, there are no laws that say you must keep your room tidy, or that you shouldn't push in front of someone to get into the movies or onto the elevator, or take all the cookies for yourself out of the jar! This is because moral rights play their part here. It's wrong to be messy, pushy, selfish, and greedy. It makes life harder for others. You and everyone else have a moral obligation to *respect* the rights of others. Moral rights are an unwritten code of social conduct where your behavior and your needs and wants must be restrained by respecting the rights of others. No one wants to be pushed out of line, to find no cookies in the jar, and your parents have better things to do than clean up after you all the time. If you are sometimes called 'greedy,' 'lazy,' 'pushy,' or 'selfish' by someone else, then you are probably violating someone else's moral right. Unless, of course, you are trying to get back at them for some injustice. If that's the case, you should talk to them about it since two wrongs (like stealing all the cookies because you're mad at your sister) doesn't make things turn out right.

Parents have several obligations and responsibilities toward their children. These rights for children include: the right to be properly fed and cared for, to be educated, to be treated by a doctor when they are sick.

Children also have a right to humane treatment: they should not be treated cruelly or forced to work at hard labor. Less than two hundred years ago children could be sold like slaves by their parents, or hired out to work long and hard hours. Now there are child labor laws which protect children from such exploitation and abuse. Less than one hundred years ago, black Americans were still treated as slaves and were bought and sold like cattle: they had no rights. Even further back in human history, in ancient Rome, wives and children were the "property" of their husbands and fathers. A man could sell his wife or kill any of his children if he wished, without any penalty, because at one time, there were no laws to protect the rights of women and children. Today, women and children are much better off in most parts of the world, but not animals. Animals are often regarded as someone's property, and the owner or master can do almost anything s/he likes without violating the law, because there are few laws to protect animals, and they are poorly enforced.

So there are some laws that protect your rights and mine, and there are a few (and we need more) to protect the rights of animals.

There are many rights that our animal kin should be accorded. These include the right to life, to humane treatment, to freedom, and to responsible care.

Living in nature, wild animals don't go around giving each other various rights. But we do see animals respecting each other's rights quite naturally. A big dog will respect the home territory of another much smaller dog. A wolf will not steal food from another weaker or younger pack mate. Such respect for another's rights is determined partly by heredity: deeply ingrained instincts. Learning from parents and others is also important. A young wolf learns to respect the rights of other wolves just like a young person learns not to be selfish, and grows up to respect the rights of other people.

Most rights are not absolute though. This means that you

Fig. 1. A father wolf gently but firmly pins one of his cubs to the ground to teach it respect for superiors. Photo by M. W. Fox.

can't always have your own way. Sometimes you must forego your right to do as you please, to watch some TV program or whatever, in deference to someone else's right. Rights, in other words, are often relative. For example: you have the right to have fun, but it should not be at the expense of others. Parents, or brothers or sisters, may want some peace and quiet or would prefer to watch another program or listen to the stereo. If they *always* get their own way, then your right to have your own way or choice sometimes, is being violated. The same rule applies if you always get your own way . . . what about the rights of others?

It might seem acceptable to let a pet dog or cat run free, but it's right to be free isn't absolute. A freedom-loving pet, just like you and me, can't always have its own way: partly for its own good, because it may get hit by a car, and partly to protect the rights of other people who don't want someone else's pet fighting with theirs or making a mess in their gardens.

All animals, including humans, share the basic right not to be made to suffer, and we will discuss this in the next chapter. There are other rights but they vary, just like some of yours do in relation to the rights of other people. A crow has the right to crow as much as it likes because it is a wild animal, but pets and children don't have the right to make as much noise as they like because it can upset neighbors. These are the *social* restraints or limits that are placed upon certain rights. While there are no limits on your right to life, there are social limits placed upon your rights to liberty and the pursuit of happiness. In seeking your own freedom and pleasure you must consider the rights of others.

There are also *ecological* or *environmental* restraints upon some of your rights as there are on animals' rights. For example, it is wrong for anyone to pollute a lake or destroy a forest, not just because it is bad for human health or other human interests. It is wrong because such actions violate the one most important right of all—the *right of all life to a whole and healthy environment.*

Sometimes the right to life of animals has to be sacrificed in order to protect the environment. This is why, when there are too many deer, they may have to be "culled," reduced in number or else they will overgraze and destroy the place where they live. If that were to happen, then even more deer would suffer, and other animals that live there too. Very of-

Fig. 2. Is it wrong to pollute a lake? What right does this violate? (The right of all life to a healthy environment). Photo by J. Dommers.

ten such imbalances in nature have been caused by man, and there may be better solutions than having to cull deer every few years. One solution, for example, is to reintroduce wolves, mountain lions, and lynx to an area in order to control the deer, since these predators were removed long ago in many places by farmers, hunters, and trappers.

Wild animals are controlled by a variety of forces—the balance of nature—which insure that the right of all life to a whole and healthy earth will not be broken. People, with their technology and power, are in many ways outside of these controlling forces. We can alter the environment, for better or for worse, like no other animal can. We have bulldozers, dynamite, chainsaws, and all kinds of things to change the environment. Blocking a river with a huge dam can alter a large area of wilderness, as can the felling of thousands of trees. No other animal on earth has this power. We need to be responsible to control this power, because we could destroy so much, and then it would be too late to correct the damage: to heal the earth. This is why we have to make the conscious effort to obey the one absolute right to keep the world whole and healthy. Even though we are so powerful, we have no right to treat animals or use nature for whatever purposes we like if those purposes violate this one absolute right. When people uphold this one right, they act as humane stewards of planet earth, and not as exploiters or parasites. If people don't respect this one absolute right, they will make life difficult if not impossible for themselves and other living things. What's best for nature, is best for us and all life in the long-run.

Humans have to develop social and ecological restraints, since without them, we can get out of control. If a human cuts down all the trees on a hill for the timber, s/he destroys the homes of millions of animals. If s/he doesn't just cut a few trees and plant new seedlings, when the rain comes, the soil will wash away and soon there will be a desert. Trees hold the soil and moisture, and without them, the environment will quickly become a dead place where few things can grow or live, including us. Animals are naturally controlled by instincts and the balancing forces of nature. Humans are relatively free from such inborn controls. What is the price of this freedom? It is the great responsibility of taking care of our planet. If we do not respect the one right of all life to a whole and healthy environment, and the rights of wild animals, plants, lakes, and all natural things *to live and to be,* we will surely destroy the natural world. And that would be a hard and unhealthy world for those of us who survived. So by respecting and upholding these rights, we are doing what is best for all creatures and all people as well. An animal (and that means us) who destroys its environment will ultimately destroy itself. In 1854, the American Indian Chief Seattle wrote to the President of the United States, Franklin Pierce (who wanted to buy large tracts of land from the Indians and grant them Reservations later, see page 167): "What is man without the beasts? If all the beasts were gone, man would die a great loneliness of spirit. For whatever happens to the beasts, soon happens to man. All things are connected."

CHAPTER 2

The Right to Life

Do all animals have the right to live? They certainly should simply because they exist, although there are some exceptions.

Under the Endangered Species Act, certain wild animals such as the tiger, bald eagle, and wolf have their right to life protected by the law. Many species are protected under this act because they are on the verge of extinction. No one is allowed to kill them or to sell or buy any products that are made from them, such as a coat made of leopards' skins or a carved ivory ornament made from elephant tusk. Poachers, people who kill these animals for profit, and illicit dealers ignore this law.

If all animals have a right to life, then do they not have a right not to be killed and eaten? The right not to be eaten is a relative one. For example, it is quite natural for a wolf to kill a deer, or a fox to kill a rabbit or field mouse. If wolves, foxes, and other animals—called predators—didn't do this, the balance of nature would be upset. Predators kill only what they need, and in doing so, they prevent the animals that they consume from becoming too numerous. If there were too many rabbits, mice, deer, and other prey, these animals would quickly eat up all the vegetation and then they would starve to death. Because there are predators who are also called carnivores, or flesh-eating animals, the vegetarian animals, called herbivores, have learned to live with

Fig. 3. The Bengal tiger is an endangered species. Is its right to life protected by law? Photo by A. J. T. Johnsingh.

them. The herbivores tend to have more babies than they need; the carnivores take the surplus and also any unhealthy or old ones.

Some animals, therefore, like the wolf and the lion, have a natural right to kill other animals for food. But what if an African lion kills a poor villager's cow or child, or a Texas coyote kills a few of the rancher's sheep? The villager's family would be in constant danger and might starve to death. The rancher could be forced out of business and suffer financially.

With a little effort, a humane solution can often be found.

Lions in Africa can be given sanctuary in a wildlife preserve and villagers can be relocated away from the lions' hunting grounds. Sheep ranchers can protect their flocks with shepherds and sheepdogs to drive coyotes away.

Even insects have the right to life, so is it right to kill them if they are becoming pests and eating up all the vegetables in your garden? Suppose your dog had fleas or worms, and you got some medicine from the veterinarian to get rid of them. What about the fleas' and the worms' right to life? All animals (including insects since they are animals too) have the right to life, but it is not an absolute right: they can't always have their own way. When an animal becomes a nuisance or a menace to us or our own pets or farm animals, we should not automatically try to kill them. We should first consider their right to life and try to find a fair solution. Because usually humans changed the environment, upset the balance of nature, and made some creatures become too plentiful we call them pests. But we created the problem and should take responsibility for a humane solution. What solutions can you think of for these examples that I have given?

Before thinking about possible solutions, let me give you one example of how we thoughtlessly destroy living things without any regard for their rights. Insects have a right to life. They all have a place in nature. Without flies, many dead things would not decay quickly and be recycled and cleaned up.* Bees pollinate flowers and without them we wouldn't have much fruit to eat. Moths and butterflies pollinate flowers and without them, the fields and woods

---

*This may seem like a selfish and human-centered justification. In other words, the insects keep the world clean for us so we accept them. This is called a utilitarian argument. I don't mean it this way. The insects are good for nature and essential for preserving a healthy world for all life, human and animal. In their way, such insects support the absolute right of all life to a whole, healthy environment don't they?

would soon become lifeless. But some people are scared of insects and they kill them if they come near or get trapped in the house. In the summer people like to leave their porch lights on; this attracts bugs, few of which will bite you. Not liking bugs, many people buy ultraviolet lights to attract the insects that get zapped and killed with an electric current. Millions can die in one night. The ethical solutions are easy once people begin to respect the rights of insects and respect their importance in nature: use a bug repellent ointment; put up a mosquito netting or screens; have a bright light in the yard or garden far from the porch to attract the bugs away from you. It's simple, and we don't always have to kill first. We must think first.

When I was in Africa one summer something happened to me that clearly demonstrates how unnecessary it is to have to kill animals that become a nuisance.

> One evening, as I was returning to my hotel room, I came across a young boy standing at the edge of a pond. He had a flashlight and a big stick, and there were several frogs that seemed to be dead at his feet.
>
> I asked him what he was doing. He replied, "I'm stopping the frogs from croaking, because they disturb the guests in the room nearest the pond."
>
> I looked at his stick and thought, "How cruel to beat the frogs to death." So I asked him, "Do you really have to kill them?"
>
> He looked at me with surprise, and said, "There's no need to kill them," and he showed me what he did.
>
> He fixed his flashlight on a big croaker, and with the stick he swept the frog out of the pond and onto the grass. The frog fell into a state like hypnosis and just lay there. The boy smiled and said, "Bwana" (meaning Sir), the frogs are *nzuri* (which means good). They crawl back into the pond after half an hour."
>
> "How beautiful," I thought, "not to kill the frogs to please the guests, as probably would be done in other

> countries." As it was, the boy was there any evening if there was a complaint about the frogs croaking. Although he might not stop them all from croaking, at least he stopped some, and without killing them.

I've thought about that boy a lot since then. Isn't there always a humane way to do everything? I'm sure there is, if we only think things out carefully.

When people first consider the animal's right to life before automatically setting out to kill it, we may benefit ourselves from not exterminating them. If we simply killed them, we could upset the balance of nature and cause even more problems. For example, a farmer once lost a calf one winter to a hungry coyote. So he waged war on all the coyotes on his ranch and poisoned and trapped them until they were all

Fig. 4. Coyotes dead from eating poisoned meat. Did the rancher have the right to kill all those coyotes? How might he have avoided this? Photo from H.S.U.S.

gone. Within no time his ranch had a plague of jack rabbits and field mice. Normally they were kept down by coyotes. The farmer, in killing his ally, the coyote, created an even more serious problem. The rabbits and mice ate up and destroyed the grazing land, his cattle starved, and he lost a fortune . . . all for the price of a calf.

Had the farmer first respected the coyote's right to life, he might have stopped and considered alternatives. The coyote was hungry: coyotes were there long before he came with his cattle. He should have tried to live in harmony with them. The farmer would have given up his right to not lose some of his stock if he had known what an ally the coyote was to him in controlling the number of rabbits and mice.

Knowing this and accepting the coyote's right to live on his land (since they were there first)* no farmer would wage a war on coyotes for the loss of a calf or two.

Sometimes though, wild animals can be much more of a pest than a coyote taking one or two calves. They do not become pests naturally, because in the wild they are controlled by the balance of nature. But when we create something unnatural, like a huge field of wheat or a range full of sheep, insect pests, even deer and starlings, will raid the crops, and mountain lions, wolves, and coyotes may take the sheep. We create the pest problems in the first place.

The usual answer to pest problems has been to use pesticides to keep insects off our plants and many insects are now resistant to DDT and other insecticides. Most of these insecticides are also harmful to wildlife and to consumers. To shoot or poison the deer, birds, coyotes, and other predators of our agricultural land and farm livestock are also common practices.

There are other alternatives to killing. Wise farmers now

---

*Parents and teachers may wish to use this issue as a point of departure to consider the rights of American Indians.

plant different crops in a cycle (crop rotation) and this helps keep the bug population down. Organic farmers avoid using any poisonous chemicals and instead encourage certain plants and insects which control other weeds and insect pests. Other farmers only rarely use pesticides. This is called integrated pest management and is better than spraying the crops repeatedly with chemicals, many of which can cause cancer and birth defects in humans.

Some ranchers now use sheep dogs as guards or shepherds instead of simply turning the sheep loose on the range to fend for themselves. Coyotes keep away and don't need to be killed. By not killing coyotes, the rancher also avoids accidentally killing other creatures with poisoned baits and traps—badgers, skunks, bobcats, eagles, hawks, foxes, and other creatures that help keep the ranchland free of rodents, and otherwise healthy.

Respecting wild animals right to life and trying to find solutions that will not violate this right, helps people in the long run because what's best for nature (the ecosystem) is best for us as well. We all need a whole and balanced environment in order to be healthy and prosper.

I still haven't given you an answer to the problem of killing the worms that your dog (or even you) may have. Sometimes we must take life in order to protect life or to improve the health of others who are sick. But it is best to find ways to prevent having to kill any creature in the first place.

The health of the body is a delicately balanced state, like the balance of all the animals and plants living in nature. If one upsets the balance and endangers the lives of others in the wild, natural forces will usually control it. Most veterinarians won't give strong antibiotics to get rid of certain bacteria in your dog if it is otherwise fairly healthy. But if your dog is made sick by these organisms—in other words the ecology or healthy balance of its body is upset—then the bacteria should be controlled. We, like dogs and other animals, have all kinds of bacteria and other things living on our skin and in our digestive systems. They help us keep healthy. They are part of the ecology of our bodies. Just imagine, billions of creatures are living on you and inside you, just like bigger creatures live inside and on the earth. You are like a small world to them. When you get sick, some of these microscopic organisms may multiply and aggravate your sickness. Then the doctor gives you medicine to help check the numbers and restore the natural balance. If the medicine killed them all in your digestive system or on your skin, you would probably die. So whenever we have to kill living things to restore the health of the body or the environment, we must be very careful not to be too destructive and seriously disrupt the natural balance.

We, therefore, like the wolf, who has the natural right to kill deer in order to live (since he can't eat what the deer eats), also have the right to kill in order to protect our health and lives, but within reason, or we may make ourselves or the environment sicker than ever!

In chapter 7 we will talk about how far we can go with killing animals and making them suffer for our health, when we look at our right to use animals in medical and other research. We can't go too far in upholding our right to health at the expense of others.

But what about our right to kill other animals for food (like the wolf kills deer) in order to live? Do we *have* to kill animals for food in order to live? We are not like the wolf, who is a carnivore. We are omnivores, which means we can eat (-vore) all things (omni-). Since we *can* eat all things—fruits, vegetables, and cereals, as well as meat—is it right for us to eat animals? What about their right to life?

There are lessons from other omnivores that can be helpful for us. Wild pigs and bears are omnivores who eat fruit,

Fig. 5. The right to life is relative. This photo shows the remains of a deer killed by Indian wild dogs (or Dholes). Why is such killing ecologically sound? Photo by M. W. Fox.

cereals, vegetables, and some meat, including the remains (called carrion) of prey killed by other animals, carnivorous predators such as the lion and wolf. Omnivores can't and don't eat too much of one thing otherwise they would upset the balance of nature. The same holds true for human omnivores. If we eat too much meat, we upset the balance of nature. Since there are so many of us, like there are more deer and other herbivorous or vegetarian animals than there are wolves—we should eat more like the deer and less like the wolf by consuming more vegetarian type foods and less meat. When millions of farm animals are kept and raised for us to eat, a lot of land and water is needed to raise food to fatten them. This land was once wilderness, full of wildlife. Therefore, the more meat people eat the more wild animals are exterminated and pushed into extinction, which is surely a violation of their right to life and to a whole and healthy environment.

The great prairies in the US, once teeming with wild animals—buffalo, antelope, and wolves—have almost all gone. The tropical rainforests of South America and jungles of Africa are fast disappearing, one reason is to raise more cattle for export to the US and Europe, especially for the fast-food hamburger industry. Thousands of unique species of wild animals and plants (some of which could be of great medical, industrial, and nutritional value to us) are being exterminated. The Earth's climate is being seriously disturbed as a consequence, causing droughts and famines in various parts of the world. What we choose to eat, therefore, affects the balance of nature and the quality of the environment. Consequently many people are now becoming vegetarians.

People also avoid eating meat for other reasons that we will discuss in later chapters.

CHAPTER 3

The Right Not to Suffer

All people, children included, have a basic right not to suffer unnaturally under the power or control of another. Animals also have this right. You don't like to be hurt or teased, neither does an animal, and many do suffer in ways that we do. How do you let others know when you are suffering? How does an animal? Animals will scream, growl, bite, scratch, claw, or whine, tremble, and try to escape when they are afraid or in pain. We too will often react this way.

You can often tell from the way a cat or dog behaves when it is suffering. They can tell us with their body language and by the sounds that they make. But how about other animals—lizards, birds, worms, fish, and the like. Some don't seem able to tell us that they are suffering. It would be like you not being able to tell someone else what you are feeling or thinking. Can you remember how difficult it was before you could talk, or when only your parents or brother or sister could understand what you were saying?

When a worm gets cut in half by a spade or when an insect gets part of its body squished under your foot, it squirms and struggles but we can't really tell if it is suffering or not. Even scientists with all their equipment, tests, and knowledge can't tell if some animals can suffer or not (see Addendum). Since we really don't know if insects and cold blooded animals like worms really suffer, we should be care-

Fig. 6. Many carnivores and primates have similar expressions which communicate how they feel. Here, the author and a maned wolf both display a grin of greeting and friendly intention. Photo by Eva Rappaport.

ful not to injure them because they *may* suffer. Just like it is impossible to tell what another person is thinking, and often difficult to tell what grown-ups are feeling, so it is impossible to tell what some animals are thinking and feeling. If we can't know, then we should not assume that an animal can't feel or suffer. This is just the same as when you can't tell what one of your friends is feeling or thinking, you don't conclude that your friend can't think or feel!

Warm blooded animals like opossums, rats, cats, pigs, and horses have brains similar to ours. They have the same pain-registering centers and pathways in their brains that we have. When they experience pain, such as a bite from a predator or the steel jaws of a leg-hold trap, they will try to escape to avoid further injuries. Pain serves a purpose: it makes an animal protect its body from injury. If animals didn't feel pain, they wouldn't survive long. What would happen to you if you couldn't feel pain?

Fig. 7. A wolf being scared into giving an aggressive snarl for a movie. The animal can't pretend, like a human actor. Is it right to treat the wolf this way just for our entertainment? Photo from H.S.U.S.

Since all animals must be able to feel pain in order to survive, and because they flee from anything that might injure them, it is quite obvious from their behavior that they don't like to be hurt.

So even if we can't tell how much pain an animal is feeling when it is in a steel-jaw trap we can tell from its behavior that it is suffering both pain and fear. If you were in that trap and you couldn't talk and tell me how much it hurt, I would still know, at least approximately. How could I know? From your behavior—your screams and yells. I can also put myself in your place. I can *imagine* what it would be like to be in your skin. When you put yourself in someone's place and imagine how they are feeling, that's called empathy.

Worrying about the possibility of being hurt is called *anxiety*. That is another form of suffering that we and other intelligent animals like cats, dogs, and monkeys can be burdened with.

You don't like to be hurt, neither do I. Since we are animals, it is logical to expect that other animals don't like to suffer either. How do we know that? Because we are animals too. This is where empathy comes into our relationships with animals.

Since there are many different kinds of animals, they will suffer differently, some more, others less. Being alone in a dark room doesn't upset me, but I know some people who are afraid of the dark. One of my friends hardly feels a thing at the dentist while I hurt as soon as I feel the drill! You and I may differ greatly in what makes us suffer and how much we suffer, and it is the same with animals. We can't say that one kind of animal species suffers more or less than another. Suffering is suffering, and when it comes to animals who can't always let us know clearly what they are feeling,

Fig. 8. Puppies (just like children) enjoy being cuddled and comforted. This feeling for others is called empathy. Photo by R. Durham, H.S.U.S.

we should treat them humanely just in case they may suffer more than we think possible.

Some animals, when they are in pain or are afraid, don't seem to show any response at all. They remain still and silent, like an opossum playing dead. It is difficult to know if they are suffering because they don't make a commotion. They act this way because they don't want to draw attention to themselves. By so doing, they avoid the risk of attracting a predator who might kill them. This inborn, or instinctive, response occurs sometimes when an animal is caught in a trap—it freezes with fear. Because it isn't struggling and screaming, it gives the impression that it isn't suffering, which is quite wrong.

Some people think that animals are just like machines and that their actions when they are injured are simply automatic reflexes. When you burn your finger, you pull your hand away. That is an automatic reflex action. You feel pain; you suffer just like an animal. So why do some people think that animals are as unfeeling as machines? Probably so they don't feel guilty or responsible when they make them suffer or see them in distress.

Other animals, especially the predators (wolves, foxes, and cats) and the primates (chimpanzees, gorillas, and baboons) don't hide things so much. They can afford to show they are suffering either because their companions will help them or because they don't have to worry about getting caught by a predator. A hurt or scared baby fawn will freeze and play dead, while a scared or injured baboon or wolf cub will scream and howl.

No person or animal wants to suffer, nor should they. But some suffering is unavoidable. It's part of life, like having a tooth ache or being anxious about something. A deer suffers while it is being chased and killed by wolves, and a wolf may suffer injuries from the hunt. This is *natural* or unavoidable suffering.

Unnatural suffering refers to the kind of animal suffering that does not occur in nature. We only see it in the various ways humans treat other animals. Wild animals that are caught in steel-jaw traps, pets that are abandoned by their owners, and farm animals that are not properly cared for, are all being subjected to unnatural suffering. Their basic right not to suffer unnaturally, and their right to humane treatment, are not being upheld.

It is sometimes argued that such unnatural suffering is es-

Fig. 9. Although it may not seem to show it, this squirrel must be suffering in the steel-jaw trap. Its basic right not to suffer unnaturally has been violated. Photo by E. Cesar, H.S.U.S.

sential for human good. That doesn't make it natural suffering, like the wolf benefitting from the deer. We have an obligation to animals to avoid unnatural suffering and a responsibility to find humane alternatives. If there's no alternative to catching wild animals for their fur than a painful steel-jaw trap, then we shouldn't wear furs and trappers should find another job. But should we kill animals humanely, even if it's just for their fur?

It is generally not *essential* for our survival for us to make animals suffer, while in nature this may be unavoidable for the wolf and lion in killing other animals for food.

Animals therefore should never be made to suffer for our pleasure or profit. This includes many uses of animals, ranging from zoos and rodeos to factory farms and trophy hunting. We will look into these problem areas where animal rights need to be recognized, later in this book. Animals must have rights because we use them in many ways and therefore have obligations towards them. One major obligation is to give them humane consideration at all times.

Addendum

Scientists have recently discovered that earth worms just like humans and other mammals, produce pain-killing substances in their bodies when injured. These morphine-like chemicals are called enkephalins and endorphins. So presumably even earth worms feel pain and have sense to avoid being injured.

All mammals, birds, reptiles, amphibians, and bony fish (but not the cartilaginous ones like sharks) have another chemical system in their brains called the benzodiazepine receptor system. This system is blocked by drugs like valium that are given to humans and by veterinarians to cats and dogs to help alleviate anxiety. So we can conclude that all these creatures—from guppies and frogs to chickens and hogs—probably experience the feeling as dread or terror.

CHAPTER 4

The Right to Humane Consideration

There is a law in every state which protects animals from being treated inhumanely. This anti-cruelty law means that society believes that animals do have a right to humane treatment. A person who mistreats an animal, such as not feeding a horse adequately in the winter, beating a dog or not providing it with veterinary treatment when sick, could be prosecuted under the Cruelty to Animals Act. In my experience though, people are rarely deliberately cruel to animals. I remember that once, when I was a boy, I got into a fight with another boy who I saw throwing rocks at a horse. He told me later that he really didn't intend to hurt or scare it. He just wanted to see what it would do. This is like someone pulling the wings off a fly to see what it will do. Do you think it is right for anyone to injure an animal to satisfy their curiosity? More often people are ignorant or indifferent, rather than deliberately cruel, like the man who didn't bother to attend to his horse's bad teeth. The poor animal was unable to eat and almost starved to death.

Although it is illegal for people to engage in dog fights and cock fights, they are held in secret in many places in the US. Pit-bull terriers and fighting cocks are specially bred and trained to tear each other apart. This is a violation of the law and of the animals' right to humane treatment. People who engage in these illegal fights say that it is natural

Fig. 10. This sick dog was rescued by a humane society officer. Its right to humane treatment and adequate care was violated by its owner. Is there a law to protect this dog's right and can its owner be prosecuted? Photo by P. Powell.

for the animals to fight, injure, and often kill each other. But this is not true, since they are encouraged to do so by being bred and trained to be abnormally aggressive.

There is also a law to protect Tennessee Walking Horses

from a practice called "soaring." In order to make them trot smartly for competition, burning ointments are applied to their skins and even pieces of glass put in their feet. Another thing that is done to horses, but is not yet illegal in America, is doping racehorses for a race. A lame horse that should be given rest and proper treatment is given drugs to feel no pain in an injured leg so that it will race. Racing on a bad leg can make the injury much worse. Sometimes these horses stumble and fall on the track and have to be destroyed.

All of this is done for money. Some people think making money is more important than an animal's right to humane treatment. What do you think? Are animals simply commodities for us to exploit for profit?

In England it is against the law to crop a dog's ears to make them pointed and stand upright, because it is considered inhumane and unnecessary for the dog's well-being. But in America this is still done on Doberman pinschers, Schnauzers, Boxers, and other breeds, when they are puppies. The ears are one of the most sensitive parts of a puppy's body. Even when their ears are cropped while the animal is asleep and feeling no pain because it has been given an anesthetic, the ears hurt afterwards.

The right of animals to humane treatment is not respected in other ways. On many modern farms, called factory farms, animals are not always treated humanely. Millions of fattening pigs and hens that lay eggs are overcrowded in small pens and wire cages. Baby veal calves are kept chained up in narrow crates for three or four months before they are sent for slaughter. Sows are often kept this way too. The calves are given only a liquid diet and no hay or grass to eat so that they are anemic and flesh will be pale. Farmers treat the animals in these ways not because they are cruel people but because they believe that these are the most efficient and profitable ways to produce meat and eggs. But there are

Fig. 11. 'Battery' caged laying-hens overcrowded in small cages. Their right to humane treatment is not considered, since giving them more space might increase the costs of egg production. Photo by M. W. Fox.

more humane ways that some farmers would adopt if people would pay a little more for their produce. Beef cattle are crowded into large pens called feed-lots where they are fattened for slaughter. They are rarely given any shade or shelter. They have certain operations performed on them, like having their horns cut off, without being given a pain-killing anesthetic, and they are branded with red-hot irons that badly burn their hides.

If anyone treated a pet cat or dog like these animals on the factory farms, they could, if caught, be prosecuted under state anti-cruelty laws. But a farmer wouldn't be prosecuted because farm animals have almost no legal protection. In the

Fig. 12. Pigs being fattened in a 'finishing' pen are often overcrowded and suffer from being so tightly packed together. Their tails have been cut off to stop them from biting each other. Photo by M. W. Fox.

eyes of the law they are not as important as pets. This isn't fair because their capacity to suffer and experience pain is not any less than a cat or a dog.

In some zoos, especially the small road-side zoos, wild animals are frequently kept in small and dirty cages. While the conditions are rarely better than on some factory farms, owners of zoos who don't take adequate care of their animals can be prosecuted for cruelty.

One popular spectator sport is the rodeo. Cowboys ride brahman bulls, bucking broncos, and lasso steers and calves. Because we are used to rodeos, like the Spanish are accustomed to bullfights, we tend to be blind to the cruelty that frequently occurs. Broncos have bucking straps pulled very tight under their groins to make them buck. When running calves and steers are roped and pulled to a dead stop with a rope around their necks, they get hurt. They may crash over and bruise themselves and sometimes they even break a horn or leg.

Fig. 13. Steer 'busting' causes suffering when the steer crashes to the ground. Is it necessary suffering? Illustration from H.S.U.S.

This is an example of a traditional sport that ignores the right of animals to humane treatment. It should be cleaned up or abolished. Another example of a traditional inhumane sport is the British fox hunt, where a pack of hounds and people on horses delight in chasing a little fox until it is exhausted. Then the hounds tear the fox to pieces. However some people enjoy a "drag" hunt where the hounds follow the *scent* of a fox instead of a live fox. A sack of fox excrement is dragged over the countryside before the hounds are released. This is a good example of a humane alternative: the horse, people, and hounds can still enjoy the chase, the fox is spared and tradition is preserved.

By far the most widespread violation of animals' rights to humane treatment, other than modern factory farming, is the annual trapping of hundreds of thousands of wild animals. They are usually caught in steel-jaw traps that hold them by one leg. Sometimes the animal will chew off its foot in order to escape. If the trapper doesn't check his trapline every day, or can't get out because of bad weather, the

Fig. 14. Calf-roping in rodeos can cause unnecessary suffering. Is this justifiable for people's enjoyment? Photo from H.S.U.S.

trapped animal suffers for a long time. Helpless in the trap, it may be killed by another animal, starve or even freeze to death. Wild animals such as foxes, raccoons, bobcats, lynx, and coyotes are trapped this way for their fur, so that people can make money and others can look nice in a fur coat. Beavers drown in traps set under water. People who wear fur coats are helping support a cruel industry. When they wear wild furs, they are showing their ignorance and lack of concern to everyone. Look out for children's toys and dolls made from animal fur, and pom poms, mittens, ear muffs, and fur-trimmed parka hoods. They could come from a coyote, raccoon, or other wild animal and I'm sure you would not like to be wearing a piece of it knowing how the animal suffered. Seal fur is also popular for making parkas, dolls, and other items. Much of this comes from baby seals who lie fat and helpless on the ice and are clubbed to death. Some furs, like mink, rabbit, and chinchilla, come from animals raised just for their fur (called pelts) on fur ranches. Do you think it is right to raise and kill an animal just for its pelt?

The right to humane treatment means that an animal should be properly cared for if it is domestic or wild, in captivity. But doesn't a wild animal have a right to be free instead of being kept in a small cage? We will discuss this right in the next chapter.

The right to humane treatment also means that an animal should not be subjected to pain or made to suffer. Suffering can range from being deprived of companions, to not having anything to do all day because it is either chained up, like a factory-farm animal, or is housed in a barren cage, as in many zoos.

Millions of wild and domestic animals are used in research—dogs, cats, rats, guinea pigs, monkeys, and others. They are given some protection, under the Federal Animal

Fig. 15. A coyote caught in a steel-jaw trap which cut his leg down to the bone. The coyote's expression is one of fear and helpless submission. Photo by Dick Randall H.S.U.S.

Welfare Act. However, in many experiments, pain and suffering does occur and their rights are clearly violated. Sometimes, but rarely, this is justified. Since the use of animals in research is a very special category, we will discuss their rights, and our right to inflict pain and suffering, in a later chapter. Next, we will consider a very important right of animals—the right to be free.

The Right to Freedom

Jeremy Bentham, a famous Englishman who lived a long time ago, said that the basic rights of all people are life, liberty, and the pursuit of happiness. Since people are animals, how appropriate would these rights be for *other* animals? We have already discussed the right to life, which is the most basic right of anything that lives. There are many conditions and circumstances that make the right to liberty less absolute than the right to life. For example, no one can have absolute freedom (even though it may seem fun) to drive their car on the sidewalk or take whatever they like from a store. There are many legal social restraints that come from having to respect other people's rights that make liberty or freedom a *conditional* right. This means that you can be free as long as you don't forget other people's rights.

Don't forget that in Jeremy Bentham's time slavery was still common in America, so when he said it was everyone's right to liberty, he meant also that no one should be kept as a slave. But how about putting someone in prison today—isn't that a violation of that person's right to liberty? It is, but criminals who are found guilty have to give up this right for two reasons: as a punishment and to protect other people's rights.

This book is about animals, so how do you think they fit into this picture? What about their right to freedom?

A lot of people think that wild animals have the greatest freedom of all life on earth. But they don't. Many have to obey rules such as territory: they must stay in their own place and not trespass on another animals "property." They have to obey rules of the social hierarchy—the pecking order—and not get out of line. Also they have to look out for danger—human hunters and natural predators would kill them if they just ran around freely in the open.

What do you think about zoos—don't they violate a wild animal's right to freedom? Some zoos, with small and barren cages certainly do, and that is quite unfair. The animals will often pace to-and-fro (called stereotyped behavior), because they are bored and don't have enough room to run, fly, swing, or play. Better zoos do what they can to improve conditions and endeavor to meet the animal's need for freedom as best as possible. Very large enclosures are expensive. Animals that are born and raised in the zoo generally adapt better. Since they haven't been exposed to the wide open spaces like an animal that has been caught as an adult in the wild, they don't seem to suffer so much.

Some animals have to forego their right to freedom and live in zoos because they are a rare and endangered species. The places where they live in nature are being destroyed by man. A zoo then becomes their sanctuary. Is being alive and having a little freedom better than having total freedom and risk becoming extinct?

With domesticated animals we have essentially three groups: working or draft animals like horses and oxen that pull carts and ploughs; farm animals that are raised for food; pets that are kept for pleasure and companionship. We will look at pets in the next chapter. Right now our concern is about the right to freedom of draft and farm animals.

Is it not a violation of the animal's right to freedom when a farmer harnesses his horse or ox to a heavy cart or plough

Fig. 16. You will often see animals kept like this wolf, in small roadside zoos. What's wrong and what animal rights are being violated? Photo by M. W. Fox.

and makes it work all day? What if the farmer decided to take the month off because he or she wanted to be free? People would starve. Thanks to horses, mules, oxen, burros, asses, elephants, and camels, human beings around the

Fig. 17. This rare black leopard has a safe sanctuary in a zoo, but is a barren cage like this one satisfactory? Photo from H.S.U.S.

world have easier lives. Without the help of these beasts of burden as they are often called, human beings might still be in the Stone Age. While some people think this wouldn't be so bad after all, we do have an enormous debt of gratitude to the many beasts of burden who have helped millions of people for generations. Without the horse and ox, the American continent would never have been opened up by the early settlers. Without the cow or horse, great past civilizations of Egypt, Rome, and Greece may never have been created. For these reasons alone, we should always respect them and never put them to new uses that cause suffering or which violate their rights.

It surely is a violation of any animal's right to freedom to make it work day in and day out. Yet carefully raised and gently treated, many of these powerful animals do seem to enjoy their work. They get to spend the day with an understanding master, who is also their friend. Indian 'mahouts' or elephant trainers, even sleep with their co-working elephants. They treat them with great respect and tenderness, sing to them and even have special feasts and festivals in their honor. Many elephants have saved the life of their mahouts, and they will never turn on their human companions or try to escape unless they are treated without respect and understanding.

A mule, horse, ox, or elephant could easily escape or kill its master if it wished. Through understanding, patience, love, and care, early man tamed these once wild animals and brought them into the service of society. In ancient Egypt, a man would be put to death if he killed a cow or cat, and punishment for mistreating a domestic animal was severe. It was for more than monetary value that people cared so much about their working animal allies: they were regarded as sacred, as helpers given by God. Both the Christian Bible and the Jewish Talmud instruct people to take good care of their animals because they are God's gift to man. We will discuss this further in chapter 9.

While a person must work (few people are so free that they don't have to work), the animals that help them in their work should be treated with the utmost respect and kindness. Any villager in such countries as India or Ireland, if seen mistreating a horse, ox, or burro, would be scorned by friends. This is because they have more obligations to these working animals than they have most other creatures. Because we have taken away much of their freedom we have a great debt of gratitude toward them.

With the coming of machines—tractors, trucks, bulldozers and the like—especially in the Western world, draft animals have been almost completely replaced. However, most of the world's population is in undeveloped countries like India, Africa, and South America, and here you will find people still relying on animal power for their livelihood. Draft animals are superior to machines even though they are less powerful. They are much easier to maintain, they are more economical and their "exhaust" (manure) is a valuable fertilizer and fuel. We have much to thank them for, and since people have taken away their right to freedom, they are obligated to treat them humanely at all times.

Fig. 18. When a horse or other draft or work animal gets too old to work any more, some owners will let them spend their remaining years in retirement in a quiet pasture or corral. These sick and burned out horses in California have simply been discarded by their former owners and are being fattened up for a few weeks before being slaughtered and turned into pet food. This may be economically efficient, but is it right, are there no other alternatives? Photo by M. W. Fox.

Animals that are raised as a source of food for humans also have their right to freedom curtailed to varying degrees. Some farm animals live an almost natural life, such as sheep, goats, and cattle out in pastures or on the open range. Still they need to be protected from predators. The good rancher doesn't simply turn them loose to fend for themselves. He or she provides shepherds and sheepdogs or stockpeople (cowboys) to look out for them.

Many farm animals today are not raised out in the open. They are kept in yards or sheds, inside pens or cages. In this factory farming that we discussed earlier, the animals have little freedom. Sometimes they don't even have enough room to turn around, lie down easily or stretch their limbs because they are either too crowded together or else they are chained or penned in a very small space. Since they cannot choose what they eat, nor can they move into a cooler or warmer place (if the building gets too hot or cold), they depend completely upon human beings for everything.

It isn't an easy job being a modern farmer. The farmer has to be a scientist and know a lot about animal nutrition and disease prevention. The farmer also has to be an engineer to maintain all the equipment—automatic feeders, waterers, sewage disposal, and climate-control heating and ventilation systems. If one thing goes wrong, the farmer could lose a lot of animals. They would be unable to help themselves. Sometimes the ventilation system breaks down and a farmer could lose fifty to one-hundred thousand chickens from suffocation or heat stroke. It is in the farmer's best financial interests to take good care of the animals. But many farmers treat their pigs and chickens like you see in the photographs in this book (see figure 11, chapter 4 and figure 19 on the following page) because they believe it is more efficient to crowd them together or chain them up. It may be, but is it right to profit from such inhumane treatment of animals?

Unnecessary privation (depriving an animal of certain basic needs such as the need to be able to get up, lie down, stretch, and turn around easily and comfortably) often occurs when farm animals are kept either too crowded together or in stalls or cages that are too small. Related to the animal's right to some freedom is our obligation to avoid unnecessary privation. While there may be health- or finance-related justifications, making such treatment seem necessary, other farmers do give their animals more freedom. So how can such treatment be justified when there are humane alternatives?

The more we domesticate animals and make them more and more dependent upon us for all of their needs, the more

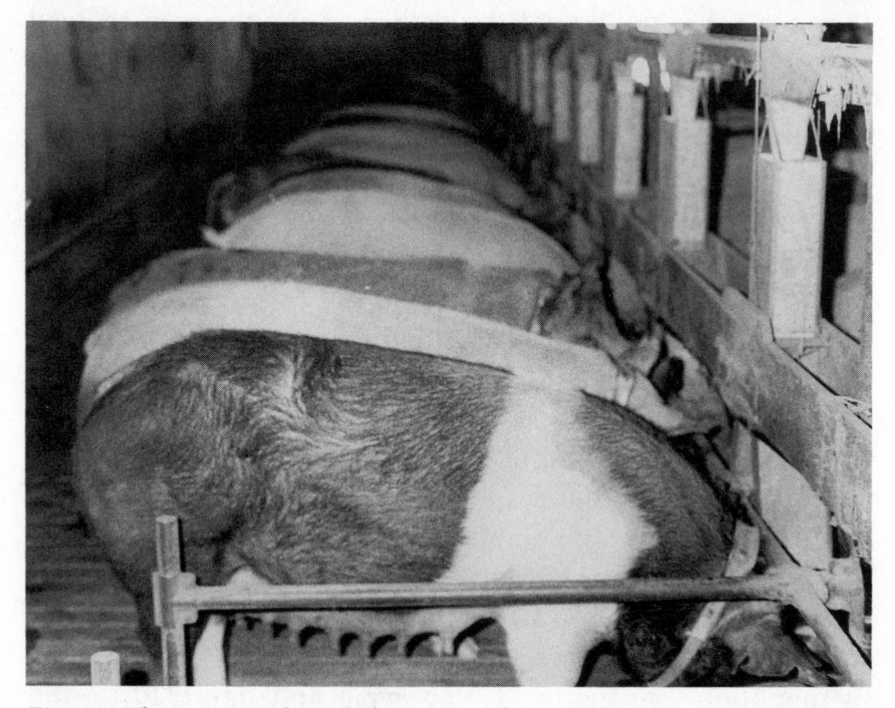

Fig. 19. These sows whose babies are to be raised and turned into pork, bacon, or sausage, are tethered to the ground in this modern factory farm. Don't they have a right to more freedom than this? Photo by M. W. Fox.

Fig. 20. This farmer keeps his pigs differently (Compare with Fig. 12). What rights are being satisfied here? Notice the cool-water sprinklers, toys, and plenty of space. Photo by M. W. Fox.

responsibilities and obligations we have towards them. This is, or should be quite independent of the farmers' need to make a profit. Generally though, a farmer who takes good care of animals is rewarded with good profits.

But some farmers are forced to cut corners for financial reasons, and they don't give the animals proper individual care and attention. The methods of animal production that they have adopted involve overcrowding and great restriction of space per animal. The animal's right to some freedom is ignored.

Fig. 21. Baby veal calves chained in separate stalls. What rights are being violated and do the benefits to humans justify keeping the calves under these conditions? Photo by M. W. Fox.

A few years ago in England, a special government commission of experts looked into this problem. On many farms, they found that the four basic freedoms of animals which they considered basic rights, were being denied. These four freedoms they defined as follows: enough space to easily and comfortably stand up, stretch, lie down, and turn around.

But are these four freedoms enough? Don't animals have more needs and rights than this? The fact that on many factory farms the animals don't have enough space to be able to even stand up, stretch, lie down and turn around easily and comfortably is shocking to most people. But it's true. Furthermore, sows and baby veal calves, for example, are frequently kept in darkness, on hard floors without any straw bedding and they are either penned into narrow crates or chained to the wall or floor so they can hardly move at all. They cannot interact with each other, play or run freely.

Why have such practices come about in clear violation of the animals' right to freedom and to humane consideration? Perhaps because some people think farm animals are dumb and don't suffer: they are just machines. Or perhaps they think such methods are most efficient and therefore profitable. But the animals do suffer and one sign of this is that diseases are very common. Animals that are not stressed and are better cared for, are physically much healthier, and don't need to be given antibiotics and other drugs (which can harm consumers) to keep them well and help them grow.

These sadly- and badly-kept farm animals on many of these modern factory farms are the new slaves of today. They certainly need to be liberated and many people, including vegetarians, philosophers, scientists, and veterinarians are working hard to change things. No person, farmer or consumer, has the right to profit at the expense of animals that are raised to feed us all. The animals' basic rights must be respected and upheld. If that proves too expensive for some farmers, then we should all become vegetarians (see Addendum) or at least eat less meat, dairy products, and eggs until more humane practices that allow the animals their basic freedom are adopted by all farmers.

Addendum

Many people are vegetarians for a variety of reasons. These include religion (Seventh-Day Adventists and Hindus); health concerns (a diet that includes meat can be a high-fat diet, and that is not good for one's health); animal welfare, animal rights, and environmental concerns. Those who eat no meat (including fish) generally call themselves vegetarians, while those who also eat no eggs or dairy products call themselves vegans. Children whose parents aren't vegetarians or vegans probably need some eggs, cheese, and fish to maintain a balanced diet and to grow strong and healthy. They should not try to become vegetarians on their own. During your growing years, your body needs more than a plate of canned spaghetti and cheese or white rice and peas. But studies have shown that meat and milk are not essential foods; people are healthier eating less or no meat and vegetables can give us all the calcium we need.

Your right to eat what you want—including sweets and junk food, isn't a right at all. Your parents have a right to feed you what they think is best for you, and if you feel like eating less or no pig, poultry, sheep or steer (i.e., pork, chicken, lamb, or beef) ask your parents to help you find nutritious substitutes like nuts, beans, lentils, whole grain rice, and tofu (made from soy beans). There are many excellent books, magazines, and local and national vegetarian societies that can help families learn how to enjoy vegetarian and vegan cuisines. Since the cost of meat products is increasing every year, and because ninety percent of all the grain grown throughout the world is fed to animals (which is a great luxury if not a waste), Americans, like people in many other countries today, are eating much less meat than a decade ago. Many people aren't ready to give up meat altogether, even though they are concerned about farm animal welfare and wildlife displacement. I call these people 'consciencious omnivores.' They do their best to avoid factory-farmed animal produce, buy from local humane and organic farmers, eat less meat in general, especially veal and pork (since calves and pigs are generally more inhumanely raised than cattle and poultry), and do their best to locate eggs from hens that are free range or aren't raised in overcrowded battery cages.

CHAPTER 6

The Rights of Pets

Like the farm animals who are wholly dependent upon man for all of their needs, so too are our pets. A rabbit, gerbil, or parakeet in its cage relies on its owner for everything, and that is quite a responsibility. We have already said that all animals, including pets, have a right to humane treatment and a right not to suffer. Their right to freedom must be satisfied as much as possible, but there are many restraints and conditions that don't make this an absolute right. Caged birds need freedom and exercise. Not only do they enjoy flitting around, but obesity is a common problem if they are not given sufficient exercise. But a caged bird flying about the house must be protected from all kinds of hazards, open doors, windows, fireplaces, pet cats, and so on. Absolute freedom for a pet hamster, gerbil, or other caged pet is also out of the question. The best way to meet their right to freedom is to give them as large a cage as possible with lots of interesting things to play with and exercise on.

A running or activity wheel keeps many rodent pets active for hours. Cylinders to crawl through and over, materials like paper and straw to manipulate, and sand or wood shavings to dig into will help compensate for their lack of freedom. Caged birds enjoy toys too—perches, ladders, ropes, bells, mirrors, and so on.

All cage pets (parakeets, mice, gerbils, rabbits, guinea pigs, etc.) with the one exception of hamsters, who prefer to live alone, should have the companionship of at least one other of their own kind. The same holds true for cats, dogs, ponies, and horses who are generally happier and healthier when given the company of their own species.

These domestic pets, by being raised in captivity and after being tamed and bred for generations to be docile, have less of a need for freedom than captive wild animals. This is one of the reasons why wild animals don't usually do well as pets. Since they are wild to begin with, they have a right to stay free in the wild and not be put in a cage for someone's selfish pleasure. If you do find a wild creature—a snake, turtle, or an interesting insect or what ever—and you must take it home, keep it only for a day *at most* to observe it. Don't forget to let the animal go in the place you found it. Because just as you have a home, a familiar place, wild animals also have a home or territory where they belong. Outside this territory they may get lost or even hurt or killed by their own kind because they are strangers and they belong somewhere else.

Orphan wild animals are another problem. They sometimes need help from humans. You should avoid the temptation of trying to make a wild young animal like a baby raccoon or fox into a pet. Pet stores and game ranches sell all kinds of wildlife as pets, and I don't advise you to get one. Many of the kinds of wild animals that are sold for pets take expert handling and care, especially when they get older. People tend to forget that the exotic wild animals that pet stores sell—parrots, ocelots, margays, and various kinds of monkeys were not born in captivity. They were taken—I prefer the word stolen—from the wild. Sometimes their mothers had to be killed first. Of those animals that are caught for the pet trade, eighty or more out of every hundred die before they reach the pet store. Buying one of the survivors is only supporting this industry, which is a clear violation of wild animals' rights to life and freedom.

For most of us, cats and dogs are the most satisfying companion animals. Their right to freedom entails a good deal of understanding, since to give them total freedom is to be an irresponsible owner. Cats and dogs should not be allowed to roam free for their own good. Free roaming cats and dogs can get lost, hit by cars, injured in fights with other animals, and they may pick up infectious and other diseases.

Free roaming pets also contribute to road accidents, they may kill wildlife, injure farm livestock, and may even bite passersby. A responsible owner keeps their cat or dog under supervision at all times when it is outdoors. Yes, cats can be leash-trained and taken for walks. Others like to play in the yard, just like a dog.

Pets have other rights which every owner should know by heart. All pets have a right to see a veterinarian when they are sick. Only too often people try to treat their pets themselves when sick. Many human medicines are not meant for animals and will do them more harm than good, and some, like aspirin and Tylenol can even poison them.

Pets have a right to proper care and attention: a clean cage or pen if they don't live free in the house; that means cleaning it regularly. Outdoor pets need shade and shelter from hot sun and cold winds. Part of meeting their right to proper care includes more than giving them wholesome food and water every day. Certain animals have special requirements: regular grooming for long-haired cats, dogs, and guinea pigs; cuttlebone for birds to nibble and obtain certain essential nutrients; a scratching post and a clean litterbox for cats; a collar and identity tag for cats and dogs just in case they get lost. Those animals that enjoy human contact and who are dependent upon people for affection and

Fig. 22. A responsible owner doesn't let a pet roam free, even if it wants to! Photo from H.S.U.S.

attention (very often because it's the only animal in the house), need to be handled and petted regularly. They need to play and they need exercise. Because cats and dogs can contract various serious diseases, they should have protective shots given by their vet and regular health checkups.

Responsible owners obey local laws too, such as using a pooper scooper when the dog defecates outside; keeping the dog on a leash outdoors; paying for a local dog license tag (the price of the license often goes to running an animal shelter which could be a safe refuge for your pet if it ever gets lost). Dog owners have to have their animals vaccinated against rabies, a terrible disease that an unvaccinated

Fig. 23. All pets have the right to proper care. This dog has been rescued from an irresponsible owner who never bothered to groom it or give it proper care. Photo from H.S.U.S.

dog could pick up from another animal and then transmit to people.

An intelligent pet has a right to some education too. All too often, a bright dog is just fed and played with and no one puts in any time to train it. Training can bring out some of the best qualities in a pet. All people who really care for their dogs will at least put them through basic obedience school. An obedient dog is easier to handle and control when necessary, such as when you are in busy traffic or when visitors come.

Part of being a responsible owner and trying to uphold pets' rights involves *understanding* the animal. This entails reading books about proper care and pet behavior. When you learn what your pet needs, feels, and is trying to communicate by way of its various actions and signals, you can better appreciate it and satisfy its needs. With dogs and cats, once you know their language you can talk to them in their own way. That's not only fun, it makes the pet more responsive and appreciative of you. It may even respect you more.

Certainly when you begin to understand what makes your pet tick you will have a deeper respect for it too. You are also less likely to get into misunderstandings. When people take time out to understand what you want or is troubling you, you feel much happier. There's nothing worse than being misunderstood—except perhaps being totally ignored! People often ignore or misunderstand their pets and even punish them when they shouldn't. For example, a young dog will sometimes piddle when it is greeting its owner. Some owners get into a rage and beat the dog, not realizing that young dogs will pass a little urine as a social signal of submission and affection. Cats like to give little nips—love bites—as a display of affection and owners who don't understand will punish them. A dog who wrecks the house or defecates or urinates indoors when left alone all day shouldn't be punished. It's trying to tell its owner that it is unhappy and frustrated about being left alone all day.

When people don't take time out to try to understand their pets, many problems will crop up. Usually the pet gets

Fig. 24. A lost, homeless, and sick dog who has lost most of its hair from mange disease. Many animals like this are simply abandoned by owners who don't really understand or appreciate pets or uphold their rights. Photo by M. W. Fox.

the hard end of the stick: it is punished, even sent to the dog pound, or abandoned somewhere. Human beings can be dumber than the animals that they think are dumb! Animals aren't dumb at all, once you understand some of their behavior. When you know what they are trying to communicate, and what their needs are, you can be a responsible owner and uphold their rights.

With pet cats and dogs it is also a responsible act to have them neutered which means fixed so they can't have babies. Life will not only be easier for them since they won't get frustrated and want to get out to mate with other animals: it will also help reduce the very serious over-population of pets. Pets need birth control. Twelve to thirteen million unwanted cats and dogs are destroyed each year in animal shelters in the US. There is no point to adding to this unnecessary and tragic waste of life.

Some parents like to have their pets have babies as a learning experience for their children. I don't think that that's right. Dog and cat owners sometimes believe that allowing their animal to have a litter of babies will help them mature or will make a nervous animal calmer. This isn't true either. Chances are the nervous pet will give birth to several neurotic kittens or puppies!

You probably know someone who spoils their pet (or child) rotten, allowing it to do as it pleases. An overindulged

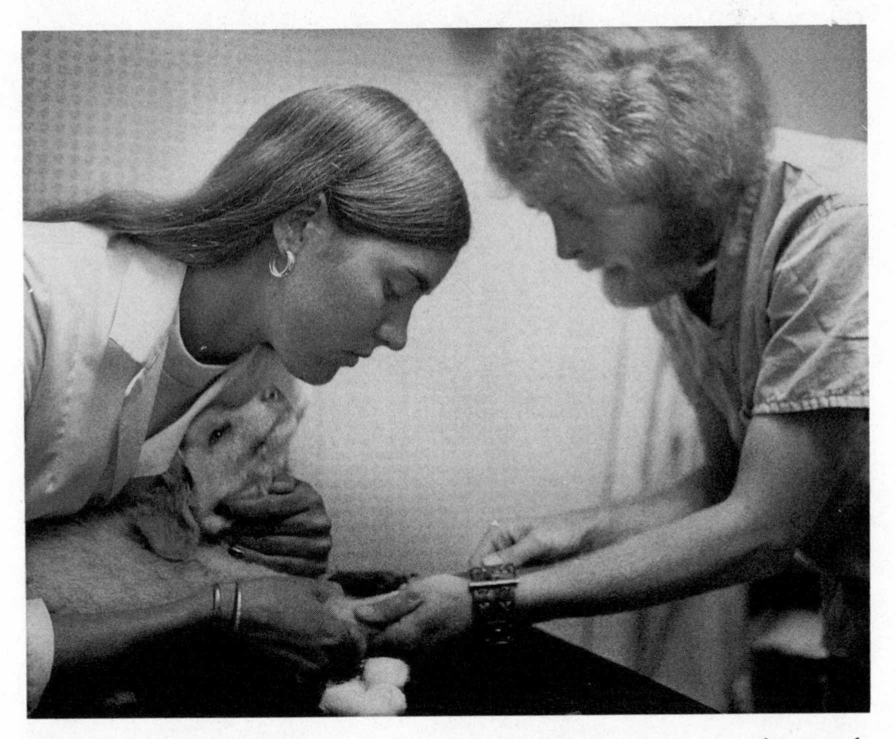

Fig. 25. Millions of unwanted pets like this puppy are put to sleep each year. Is the only solution to kill them? Photo by *The Washington Post* Co./H.S.U.S.

Fig. 26A. While one solution to the pet over-population problem is to collect them off the streets and put them in a truck and take them to the pound for adoption or destruction . . .

Fig. 26B. . . . another solution is for humane societies to visit schools and teach humane values and responsible pet ownership. Photos by M. W. Fox.

Fig. 27. Pets should not be allowed to roam free at any age. Fortunately this lost kitten was found by a humane society officer, and given a good home. Photo by H.S.U.S.

and poorly trained pet isn't nice to have around. Pets (and children) must learn to respect the rights of others. These spoiled pets often get sick, overweight and they bite their owners if they don't get their own way. People who mollycoddle their pets like this think they are doing the right thing and really know all about pets' rights. But they are wrong aren't they?

Owning a pet clearly takes more than just keeping it clean, giving it food, water, regular exercise, and the occasional cuddle. This is because pets are so dependent upon us for so much and it is our responsibility to respect their many rights. Those people who believe that a pet should be allowed to live a natural life—roaming free, breeding, and so on, think that to control their natural instincts is cruel and a violation of their basic rights. But control is necessary. That is what being a responsible owner (or parent, for that matter) means. In the process, the pet's basic rights are respected and everyone is happy.

Addendum

▪ THE TEN COMMANDMENTS OF ▪ PET OWNERSHIP

1. All companion animals should be treated humanely —with patience, compassion and understanding.
2. Every pet has the right to have certain basic needs satisfied: regular exercise, play, companionship, and grooming, as the case may be. They also have the right to a clean and quiet place to live and rest; to eat and sleep.
3. All pets have the right to receive fresh water and a complete and balanced diet each day as needed. They also have the right to receive proper veterinary treatment if they are ill.
4. All pets have the right to fulfill their lives, within the social constraints of responsible ownership; This may include the curtailment of certain needs, such as the need to roam free or breed, for the ultimate benefit of the animal, society and the environment, as the case may be.
5. A caring owner understands the animal's needs and provides those conditions most conducive to ensuring its physical and psychological well-being.

6. No person has the absolute right to inhumanely exploit an animal for profit, pleasure, or other selfish purpose.
7. An understanding owner endeavors to respect and appreciate the animal for itself, independent of personal bias and selfish wants. Such an owner attends (listens) to the animal and even when it appears to misbehave the owner endeavors to ascertain what the pet needs or is trying to communicate. No pet should be overindulged to the detriment of its physical or psychological well-being.
8. No pet owner shall physically or psychologically abuse or neglect an animal, or abandon it. The ultimate responsibility is to ensure that when the time comes, the pet will die painlessly and with dignity, if euthanasia is required.
9. Before obtaining a pet or giving one to other people, every person has the obligation to the animal to assure that it will live in a home that will best satisfy its basic needs and also that its basic rights will be recognized and upheld at all times.
10. All pet owners, and those who care for animals, have the right and responsibility to share with others, especially children, the Ten Commandments of Pet Ownership, and to intercede in defense of any animal when its rights are violated and when it is being treated inhumanely, either through intent or indifference (neglect).

CHAPTER 7

The Rights of Laboratory (Experimental) Animals

One of the most touchy aspects of our relationship with animals is the use of animals in laboratory sciences. Some people, called anti-vivisectionists, are at one extreme in their concern. They want an abolition of *all* experiments on live animals. At the other extreme there are those who say that it is quite all right for us to do whatever we like to animals. They say that God gave us such a right, since it is written in the bible (Genesis 1:26) that man has dominion over all creatures.* If what is done to the animal may produce something of educational value, adds to scientific knowledge, or can help improve human health, they argue that it is worth killing animals or subjecting them to painful experiments.

Which point of view do you feel is right? The anti-vivisectionists say we should allow no experiments on animals and the animal utilitarians, or vivisectionists, claim that we can do anything to animals if it is for the ultimate good of humanity. Perhaps they are both wrong. Much can be learned from treating animals that are already sick or injured in testing new life-saving drugs and surgical techniques. Animals, as well as people benefit from new discov-

*I believe that dominion should be interpreted as God-like stewardship of nature and showing compassion for and respecting the rights of animals. But many people act as though dominion means the right to dominate all animals and to use them for what ever purpose we wish, regardless of their rights (See Appendix III).

eries. But is it right to take perfectly healthy animals and harm them to find cures for human illnesses, many of which we bring on ourselves by poisoning the environment, eating the wrong kinds of foods, and by not adopting a healthy, active life-style?

Do people have the right to do whatever they like to perfectly healthy animals? Some say that it is acceptable for high school students to do all kinds of experiments on rats, mice, and other animals if they learn something in the process. Rats have been poisoned with lead paint, fed deficient diets that made them ill, and given electrical shocks to force them to solve problems. Hamsters have been given household chemicals to see which are poisonous, and fresh water fish are put in salt water by high school students for biology class projects or for the high school science fairs. I could go on with more disturbing examples, but I won't. The main criticism is that many of the answers that the students hope to get from their experiments are already in books and scientific articles. Doing experiments over again is a needless repetition and a waste of animals. No new information is going to be gained from such studies. Animals suffer unnecessarily and their lives are pointlessly wasted.

There are lots of valuable learning experiences that can be derived from animals without having to kill them or make them suffer. There are many humane alternatives such as observing and recording how various animals behave, interact, communicate, and develop.

For example, how does mother mouse in her cage take care of her babies? How often does she nurse and groom them? When do their eyes open and how do they play and fight with each other? What do they do when you put something unusual in their cage, like a small piece of wood, or a ball of tissue paper? What differences are there between baby mice that are handled regularly, compared to those

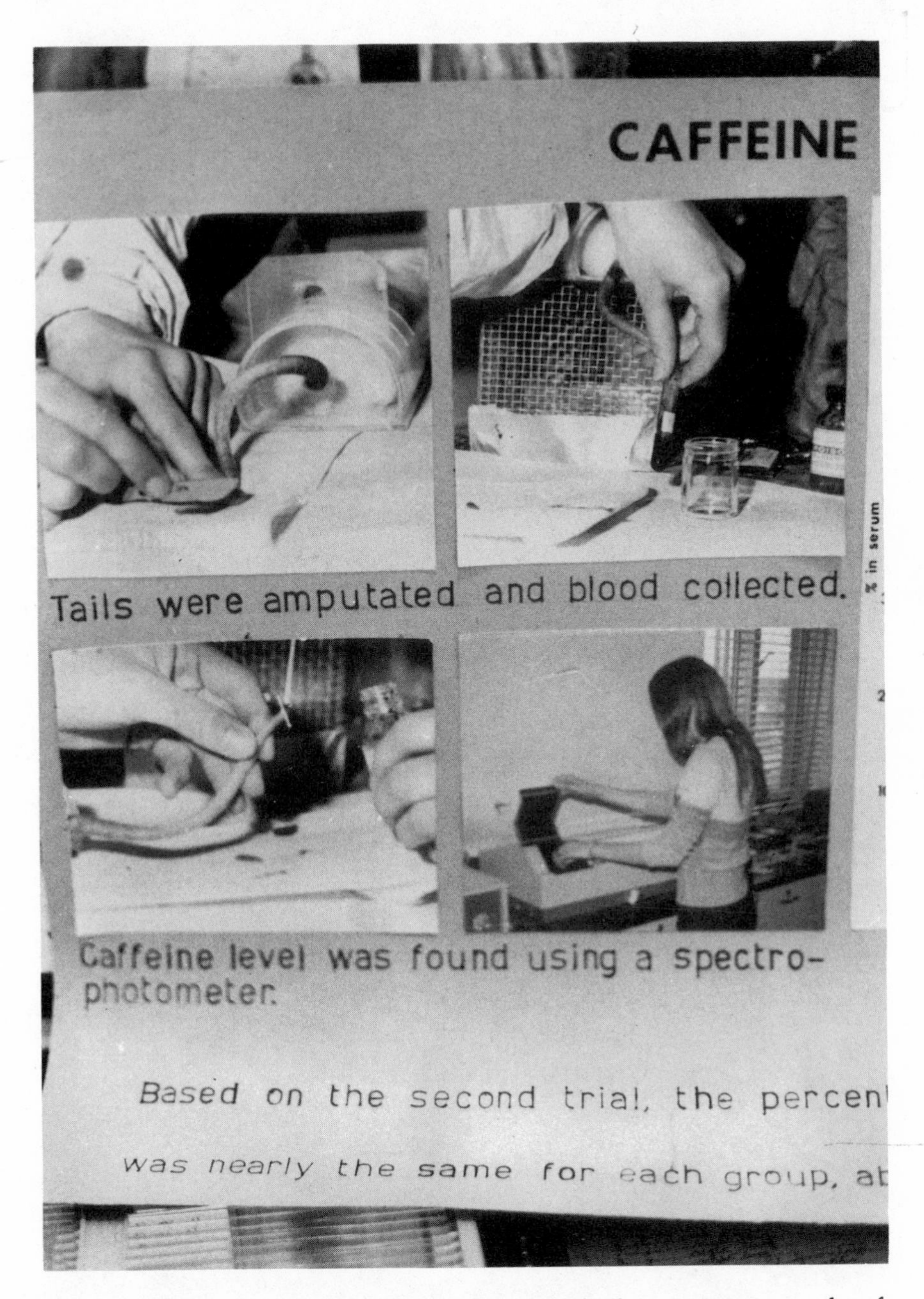

Fig. 28. Part of a high school student's science fair project: a study of the effects of caffeine on rats (a needlessly repetitive exercise). Can the suffering and death of rats be justified for a student to learn about basic scientific principles—are there no humane alternatives? Photo by M. W. Fox.

Fig. 29. This science fair project involved analyzing tape recordings of the sounds that green frogs make: a very sophisticated study which (in contrast to the one in Fig. 28) did not injure or kill any animals. Photo by M. W. Fox.

that are never petted? These are just a few examples of so-called noninterventive studies that can be done with animals in schools. You don't have to intervene—by putting them on a diet deficient in some vitamin or feeding them some poison—in order to learn scientific principles. In other words, you can learn from animals without violating their basic rights.

These kinds of studies respect the right of laboratory (experimental) animals not to suffer unnecessarily. We have an obligation to them to respect and uphold this right, but only too often it is ignored. Why? Partly because humane alternatives haven't been considered. Also because it is often believed that animals don't suffer very much. We have discussed this earlier in the book—they can and do suffer. Very often there's a kind of trade-off argument that goes like this: it's okay if the animal suffers provided the student gains by learning something. I think this is a very selfish point of view. Even worse, the student may learn not to care about animal suffering if it is justified and accepted by teachers and scientists.

There is a law that does protect some of the rights of laboratory animals. This is called the Federal Animal Welfare Act. Regulations have to be followed by scientists who use animals in research, which spell out how they should be cared for—fed, watered, transported, handled, and so on. Painful experiments on all warm blooded animals (including dogs, cats, monkeys, but not rats or mice or farm and wild animals) have to reported to the government agency that oversees this welfare act.

But there are some serious problems with the ways research animals are usually treated. One problem is defining how big the animal's cage should be. Dogs, cats, and monkeys are usually kept in small cages and they never get out for exercise and have no opportunity to interact with each

Fig. 30. By any reasonable scale, these standard research cages for monkeys are far too small. What basic needs and rights are being violated? Photo by M. W. Fox.

other. The cages in laboratories are much smaller than those in zoos. This is a violation of the laboratory animals' right to freedom. Monkey cages are not only too small, there's nothing inside for the monkeys to play with. Sometimes the monkeys go crazy and tear out their hair or just sit and rock to and fro. They aren't in a fit state to do research with, but these problems are too often ignored.

The Animal Welfare Act stipulates that pain-killing drugs should be used if the animal suffers as a consequence of some experiment. But if giving a pain-killer might interfere

Fig. 31. This is how the highly intelligent and sociable chimpanzee is kept in most research laboratories in the US. What improvements do you see that are needed? Photo by M. W. Fox.

with the experiment, then it need not be given. This is called a loophole in the law, and it should be changed.

Laboratory animals suffer too much for trivial reasons. They are made to suffer in the process of safety testing new cosmetics, household detergents, floor polish, and other things like that. These things are not essential to human health. If laboratory animals are to suffer then it surely should only be allowed where there is the promise of finding cures for human or animal diseases . . . and only then, after the scientist has searched carefully to find more humane alternatives. Often, live animals are not needed for some tests or experiments. Bacteria, plants, human cells grown in a special fluid (called tissue culture), and simple celled organisms are humane alternatives. Such living things don't suffer and in using such alternatives, the scientist can find a way to respect laboratory animals' rights not to suffer unnecessarily. Computers can also be used sometimes instead of live animals, and human volunteers can be employed in many clinical studies.

Laboratory animals are also used extensively in military research, from testing and developing new weapons, germ warfare, poisonous gases, and even radiation. It is reasoned that this kind of research is essential so that we can defend ourselves better in case of war. But is it right to make animals the victims of our inability to make peace instead of war?

Like the curious child who pulls the legs or wings off an insect to see what happens, some scientists do similar things to laboratory animals. It is strange that grown-ups often behave like children and do things to satisfy their own curiosity regardless of how much the animal suffers. It may be true that until humane alternatives are developed and people become more respectful of animals' rights, a few animals must suffer so that many animals and people may benefit by improved health and protection from disease. This may be jus-

Fig. 32. A rack of rabbits being used to test new drugs. In one test (called the Draize test) substances such as new cosmetics are put in their eyes, to see what chemical level causes the eye to burn. The rabbits suffer and sometimes they go blind. Photo by M. W. Fox.

tified by some as necessary and unavoidable suffering. Yet to make an animal suffer just to satisfy one's scientific curiosity, like the psychologist who gives electrical shocks to make cats or rats behave in certain ways without any foreseeable benefit to people or other animals, is quite wrong. People who do these inhumane things are rightly criticized by anti-vivisectionists, although not all scientists are like this. One way to stop unnecessary suffering is to ask those who make them suffer just *why* they are doing what they do. If they can't prove any benefit to alleviate suffering in humans or animals, then they must stop.

Doing cruel things to animals just to gain more knowledge or to test ideas is absolutely wrong. Yet because our knowledge is so incomplete, things aren't so clear cut as they might be. A scientist might make a sudden valuable and unforeseeable discovery at the expense of animal suffering or life: a scientific breakthrough as it is called. So it's really the responsibility of the scientist to take good care of his animals and to try to find humane alternatives. Scientists should also ask themselves: "Do I really need to know what I *think* I want to know if animals have to die or suffer in order for me to get it?" I remember being shocked by one scientist who was experimenting on a raccoon-like animal called a coati-mundi. They are very curious, playful, and cuddly animals. He had to destroy several in order to discover what nerves and muscles they use to move their long snouts. Did that man really have to know what he wanted to know? Was it worth killing those animals and making them suffer? Should laboratory animals suffer so that we can find cures for diseases and other problems that affect us humans? Why don't we use human volunteers instead? Would you like to volunteer in the place of an animal?

Some people feel that it is wrong to try to find cures for human diseases at the expense of animals, since many illnesses we cause ourselves. That doesn't mean these people care more for animals than for people. Rather, they believe that the best and first medicine is prevention.

Another serious problem is that there are too many people in the world so that in many places there isn't enough food or good land to farm. As a result, people suffer malnutrition and disease. Therefore, family planning to prevent overpopulation is another important aspect of preventive medicine.

The real aim is to improve the quality of *life:* to reduce animal and human sickness and suffering. Laboratory animals are sacrificed for this reason, but that would be a pointless waste if we do not do two things: clean up our polluted environment (in the process we would help protect and conserve wildlife and nature), and limit the growth of the human population. In other words, if we are to see any real progress in human medicine and in public health, there needs to be much less reliance on vivisection. Studies on animals should be for the benefit of *all* life, and not for someone's personal profit or curiosity. Experimental animals have helped us in countless ways: from developing life-saving drugs and making vaccines to safety-testing equipment so that man can explore outer space. We owe a great debt to them, which we can repay by being humane and considerate at all times of their basic rights.

My own thinking has led me to the point where I feel that no animal should be deliberately harmed for purely human benefit. I also believe that it is wrong to inflict disease and injuries, like burns and brain damage, on laboratory animals, and to inbreed those that have inherited disorders as models of human disorders. We should instead learn from treating animals that are already sick or injured. Scientifically speaking, these are better models to learn from that provide the added assurance that these advances would also benefit animals.

Another criticism that I have of laboratory animal research is that many human health problems aren't going to be prevented by such research. Ways of diagnosing, treating, and curing various human diseases may be found, but the best medicine is to focus on *preventing* disease. This includes good sanitation and personal hygiene; clean air and water, and wholesome food;* and an environment that is not poisoned by agricultural chemicals, like pesticides and industrial poisons. Many of these cause cancer, birth defects, and other diseases. So it does not seem right to me to use ani-

*Many nutrition experts advise us to consume less meat and fatty, processed, and junk foods. They suggest that we avoid sugar and salt, and eat more high fiber cereal grains, pulses (beans, peas, lentils), and fresh fruits and vegetables which, ideally, have been organically grown in good soil and haven't been treated with pesticides and other agricultural chemicals.

mals to find ways to treat these human diseases that we cause ourselves. Is it also right to addict animals to and poison them with alcohol, tobacco, cocaine, heroin, and other abused substances? People have a choice not to put these harmful things into their bodies, just as society has a choice not to poison the environment—our air, food, and water—with harmful chemicals; and our bodies in the process. It doesn't seem right to me to make animals suffer in research laboratories for problems that we bring upon ourselves and could therefore correct ourselves.

CHAPTER 8

Animal Rights Versus Human Interests

In the last chapter we discussed the pros and cons of respecting an animal's right not to suffer and discussed the fact that exceptions are often made to permit animals to suffer or die so that humans may benefit. This is called utilitarianism.

One way of looking at the ethics of sacrificing the rights of a few for the benefit of many is in terms of *costs and benefits*. The costs to some animals, of having to deprive them of their freedom, to kill them, or to subject them to physical pain or other suffering, has to be judged and evaluated in relation to the benefits that are gained by doing such things to them. A close look at such costs and benefits can help us determine when it is morally or ecologically right or wrong to do certain things to animals that may violate some of their rights.

Above and beyond all human and animal rights is the one and absolute right of life to a whole and healthy environment. Above all human claims over animals (to exploit them for any reason) are those animal rights of humane treatment and of not suffering unnecessarily. The right to life for animals, especially of endangered species, comes first over such human rights as the right to profit at their expense for reasons of enjoyment, sport, entertainment, or for money. This makes it wrong to trap and kill wild animals for profit or to hunt and kill wild animals for sport or for status (as trophies). Hunting should only be acceptable when it is done humanely and only then when the hunter has to kill to live and/or is helping maintain the balance of nature.

The rights of hunters, trappers, rodeo cowboys, cock- and dog-fight enthusiasts, sealers and whalers, horse racers, people who run circuses and roadside zoos, and of others who use or exploit animals for various reasons, are not rights at all. They are selfish claims to use animals regardless of the rights of those animals. How can we, and that means both grown-ups and children, change the values and attitudes of those people who cause unnecessary death and suffering to animals? Albert Schweitzer wrote in his book *The Teaching of Reverence for Life:**

> Whenever animals are impressed into the service of man, every one of us should be mindful of the toll we are exacting. We cannot stand idly by and see animals subjected to unnecessary harshness or deliberate mistreatment. We cannot say it is not our business to interfere. On the contrary, it is our duty to intervene in the animal's behalf.

There are many ways we can help animals. A first step is through education. Children who learn about animal rights are less likely to follow in the footsteps of their parents or other adults who do not respect animals' rights. A declaration listing the rights of animals was presented in 1977 to the United Nations for representatives of countries from all over the world to read and take home with them. The children's version is on p. 93. See Appendix II for the complete Declaration of the Rights of Animals.

*New York: Holt, Rinehart and Winston, 1965.

Fig. 33. & 34. Aleutian sealers clubbing and then skinning seals they have herded onto the land. What are the justifications, if any, for such killing? Photo from H.S.U.S.

Fig. 35. Circuses may not always involve animal suffering or cruelty, but the right to exploit animals for entertainment should be questioned. What do spectators learn about the animals—that they can be dominated by man and taught to perform unnatural acts? Photo from H.S.U.S.

DECLARATION BY
• YOUNG FRIENDS OF ANIMALS •

1. All animals have the right to live and be happy, like me.
2. I will not abandon any animal who lives with me because I would not like my parents to abandon me.
3. I will not harm animals; they suffer like humans.
4. I will not kill animals; killing for fun or for money is a crime.
5. Animals, like me, have the right to be free; circuses and zoos are prisons for animals.
6. I will learn to observe, understand and love animals; animals will teach me to respect nature and all forms of life.

—London, September 1977*

Another way to change people's values and treatment of animals is through legislation. This means making more laws to protect animals' rights. The main laws that exist today have been mentioned earlier in this book. Laws are valuable, but it takes a lot of effort, time, and money to get them accepted, either through Congress or the legislatures of the various states. And it takes even more time, effort, and money to enforce them. At the end of this book there is a copy of a bill drawn up to ensure the humane slaughter of farm animals. Once a bill like this is voted on and passed by members of Congress in the House of Representatives in Washington, DC, it then has to go through the Senate and be voted on by senators. If not enough money is appropriated to help pay for enough federal inspectors to enforce the

---

*After reading this book, perhaps you may want to draw up your own declaration of animal rights. If you do, please send me a copy, in care of the publisher, and I will respond to you personally.

new laws in the bill, then it won't be effective, even though everyone might have voted in favor of the bill.

A bill that passes through Congress and becomes law means that everyone in the whole country must obey the new regulations, otherwise they may be prosecuted. Bringing someone to trial to decide if they have really broken the law is very expensive for both the defendant (the one who may have broken the law) and the plaintiff, who in this case is the federal government (whose job it is to enforce the law). Both parties have to pay lawyers and other costs. Even a seemingly straightforward case of a man shooting an endangered species like a golden eagle could take years to reach a settlement. Since it is difficult to write a law that covers everything, lawyers can find loopholes in the law, so that a person might get off without being punished for the crime.

All of the various states in the US have their own laws too, and not all of them are the same as federal laws. For example, federal law says that it is illegal to engage in cock fights, but in some states like New Mexico, it is still legal. There is no federal law banning the use of the steel-jaw trap, but a few states, such as Connecticut, have outlawed their use. Such contradictions between state and federal laws should be corrected so that there will be no legal loopholes or other excuses for people who do not treat animals humanely.

Great improvements can also be made within organizations without having to go to the trouble and expense of getting new laws passed and enforced. For example, a division of the National Academy of Science and the National Institute of Health set up guidelines as to how laboratory animals should be treated. Scientists visit animal laboratories to see if the facilities and care are up to standard. The National Greyhound Racing Association has spoken out

Fig. 36. A group of young people who support their local humane society. The billboard is one way to educate the public. Photo from H.S.U.S.

Fig. 37. Teenage supporters of the humane movement, carrying placards in public protest against rodeos. Photo from H.S.U.S.

against people using live rabbits to train their dogs, and some states, like California, have made such practices illegal. As for International High School Science fairs, the regulations concerning how students should treat animals have been slowly improved over the years thanks to the pressure of local and national humane societies. Concerned citizens established a rule in California schools that no painful experiments should be done on warm blooded animals.

This is where people, concerned school children, and grown-ups alike can help animals. If we all just sit around waiting for better laws and regulations to be drawn up to help animals, little will be done. We have to be politically active: hold meetings to discuss things that concern us, from having to kill and dissect frogs in the classroom, having meat from factory-farm animals served in the school cafeteria, to trying to stop the drugging of horses, dog fights, trapping or other inhumane activities in your state. Make petitions, collect signatures, contact appropriate city, county, and state politicians, and support local and national environmental, conservation, and humane organizations.

Another strategy to bring about humane reforms to protect the rights of animals is to stage public demonstrations.

Fig. 38. A Japanese-made car stuck with harpoons: part of a public demonstration against Japanese whaling, aimed at a general boycott against Japanese goods. Photo from H.S.U.S.

Fig. 39. A poster used to draw attention to the tuna fish industry's destruction of dolphins—part of a successful national boycott against eating canned tuna fish. Photo by G. Laurish.

(This is part of your right to freedom of speech established by the first Amendment of the Constitution). A store selling the furs of wild animals could be picketed by people carrying suitable protest placards and distributing literature to passersby. This is legal under the freedom of speech, but you should first inquire about local ordinances. It may be illegal to stage a demonstration (which should always be peaceful and well-mannered): you may first have to get a permit from the police or city hall.

Another way to protest is to set up a boycott. A boycott means that people refuse to buy certain things, but it has to be well-organized and widespread, otherwise those who you are trying to influence may not feel a thing. You may have heard of the tuna fish boycott and the Japanese goods boycott. Both were set up by many different organizations all over the US. One, that tried to make tuna fishermen improve their fishing methods so that fewer dolphins would get killed in the process, was successful. The boycott was an added pressure to other strategies which eventually got the tuna-fishing industry to make improvements. There is now an International Whaling Commission made up of scientists and others that is making some progress in its efforts to save the whale.

Those of you who care for animals will find that there are all kinds of public organizations, government agencies and international commissions working hard on many of the animal problems that concern us all. A lot of people do care and are dedicating much or all of their time to helping animals and the environment. Some of the public organizations that you may want to join and support are listed at the end of this book, together with some ecological and humane guidelines for every day living. With your support, things will get better faster. It's no use simply liking animals and doing nothing else for them. Liking them is just the beginning. They need your help, because their rights must be recognized and respected by all people. This is Animal Liberation.

CHAPTER 9

Animal Liberation—Philosophy and Religion

The following statement was prepared by Dr. Tom Regan in collaboration with the author and other members of the Society for the Study of Ethics and Animals. The Society was founded during a symposium held at the Seton Hall School of Law, February 3–4, 1979.

"People should not be treated as mere things. We are not tools to be used merely for another's pleasure, profit, or curiosity. People have a life that is valuable, regardless of whether they are of use to others. To treat people in ways that deny them value in themselves is to violate their rights.

Animals too, are not mere things. They, too, have a life that is valuable regardless of whether they are of use to others. Therefore, animals have rights. To treat them as mere things, to treat them as mere tools to be used for human pleasure, profit or curiosity, is to violate their rights.

What is there about our lives that we value? Pleasure, and a minimum of pain; companionship; the satisfaction of wants and needs. These, certainly, are among the things that give value to our lives.

Animals too, have a life that is valuable in these ways. Animals too, experience pleasure and pain, have needs, wants, and they seek companionship. In these ways at least, we share a common nature with them. In these ways at least, the value of animal and human life has a common basis.

Does this mean that animals have the very same rights that people do? Must we say that they have a right to vote because we have this right? No, we need not say this. What we must say is that we have certain rights based on our common nature, especially the rights not to be made to suffer or to be killed merely for pleasure, profit, or curiosity. Yet animals are treated in these ways. In laboratories, in zoos, in school science fairs, in modern factory farms, in all these and more, animals are treated as mere things, as if they had no value in themselves.

Such treatments must be stopped, not only because it is a good thing for us to be kind to animals, but because we owe it to them. When rights are violated, justice, not kindness, is an issue. Their defenseless state—their inability to speak out for their rights—makes our duty to help them all the greater. Tomorrow they will suffer and they will be killed unless we act for them today . . . and act we must. Respect for justice requires nothing less."

What has evolved from this philosophy is an animal liberation movement which, in many ways, is like the earlier movements to liberate slaves and emancipate women. Several text books have now been written on this topic (see *Books for Further Reading*) and the subject of animal rights and humane ethics is now being taught by professors in many universities.

Even so, there are many people who still believe animals can't have rights because they can't be held morally responsible for their actions and only those who can be responsible can claim to have rights. But human babies have rights, and they are too young to be morally responsible. The mentally handicapped can't be held fully responsible for their actions, yet they have rights. So why shouldn't animals? To claim that they can't have rights is called 'speciesism' (which is like racism and sexism).

Some people have argued that animals can't have rights because they are incapable of suffering, but scientific studies of animal behavior and physiology have proven that animals can suffer, often in ways very similar to us. A dog whose human companion has died often suffers from severe depression, and many animals can be tormented by anxiety, like cats and dogs who are afraid of thunderstorms and fireworks. Some even suffer from jealousy, like the dog who acts depressed or is more aggressive when a new puppy or a baby comes into the home.

Others believe that animals can't have rights, and should not be given equal and fair consideration because they are inferior to us, since they can't talk, reason, and lack free will. Such people are ignorant about animals' behavior and recent scientific advances in the study of animal behavior, which is called ethology. Animals *do* talk to each other, using various sounds and body postures (called displays or body language) to communicate their emotions, intentions, needs, and wants. A dog who brings a leash or a ball to you, is clearly communicating a wish to go out for a walk or to play.

Studies of animals' learning ability reveal that they can think and reason, and they have insight and foresight. For example, a friend of mine baked some pastries and put them on the kitchen counter to cool. She carefully moved the kitchen stool far away from the counter so the dog couldn't jump up on it and thus reach the pastries. She came back a half-hour later to find most of the pastries had been eaten by the dog, who had pushed the stool over to the counter by herself so she could reach the delicacies. That is a clear demonstration of insight and reasoning.

Many people believe that only humans have what is called free will and animals don't have this because their behavior is automatic or instinctive, unthinking. This may be true for relatively simple forms of life such as plants, bacteria, and certain invertebrate animals like worms and insects, but that is no reason not to respect such living things. They, like us, are part of Earth's creation. Animals often express free will, like when a dog refuses to obey a command or a cat deliberately knocks items off the dresser to get its sleeping owners' attention. This is not instinctive, mindless behavior—it is willfully calculated.

Another reason why people feel that animals can't have rights is because they believe that humans are superior, being made in God's own image and having God-given dominion over the rest of creation. However, some theologians contend that to be made in God's image means that we on earth should behave like God by treating all of creation as we would have them treat us, and since we, and all other living things, have the same origin or creation, we are all equal in God's eyes. This view is expressed in Ecclesiastes (3:20), where it is clearly stated that "man hath no preeminence above a beast."

In the book of Genesis it is said that we have dominion over the animals. Some people interpret this as meaning that we are free to dominate and exploit animals as we choose. But the original meaning of dominion is from the Hebrew word *yorade*, which means to come down to; to have sympathy with. This is a clear commandment of humane, compassionate care or stewardship. This was later translated into the Latin *domino* (which means to rule over) from which the English word *dominion* is derived.

▪ Do Animals Have Souls?

There are people who believe that animals don't have souls, but the Bible clearly states that they, like us, are living souls, called *nefesh* in Hebrew. The following letter from the *Toronto Star* (June 3, 1980), entitled "Bereft teen is agonizing over a dead dog's soul," addresses this issue well:

> Dear Dr. Cotter:
> My dog has just died and I can't stop worrying about her soul. Yes, I believe she had one because she showed more intelligence and love than many people. My family tends to reject religion, so I asked some of my religious friends and teachers at school if they thought animals went to heaven. They all said animals have no spirits and that only humans go to heaven. It doesn't seem fair that brainless, destructive people could get to heaven if someone as lovely as my dog couldn't.
>
> *Answer:*
> Traditional Christianity does not say that all people go to heaven; it says that some may go to hell—for example, the destructive ones that you talk about. Do you think "bad" animals should go to hell? Is there any such thing as a "bad" animal in the moral sense?
>
> The reason why traditional Christian theology has excluded animals from enjoying heaven is that they are not considered to have "rational souls." It's a bit of a joke to suggest that human beings have rational souls, given the way they behave most of the time. The distinction is supposed to be, however, that animals do not have the habit of self-conscious reflection which can make them aware of both themselves and of God. The ability to enter God's presence totally (i.e., in "heaven") thus seems to depend on the awareness of God's being.
>
> The funny thing is that animals and plants seem to me to be very much aware of God. The real issue is probably that they do not need to be saved from sin if

> they are incapable of sin. They may well be able to enter God's presence with awareness, but they do not need Christ's cross and resurrection to bring them back to God.
>
> You have raised a very important point. I think theologians should take some sharp looks at the boundaries of consciousness in human and other beings from a theological point of view. St. Paul says the whole of creation has been moving towards the salvation brought by Christ. I think our understanding of these matters may be in for revision, and that your instinctive feeling about your dog should be attended to by believers.

It was the Greek philosopher Aristotle who established the idea that only humans have rational souls, while animals, who he believed lack the ability to reason, simply have sensitive animal souls. It was Thomas Aquinas who later extended this idea and incorporated it into early Roman Christianity. He reasoned that only humans have rational immortal souls, and that only humans, not animals, go to heaven. Yet animals are described in the Bible as living in heaven, like the great white horses in the book of Revelation.

There are clearly no religious or valid philosophical reasons for not respecting animals' rights and treating them humanely. All the major religious traditions of the world stress the importance of treating animals with compassion and respect.

Judeo-Christian tradition. In the Bible we find in Proverbs 12:10 the reminder that, "A righteous man hath regard for the life of his beast." In Isaiah 66:3 it is said, "He who kills an ox is like he who kills a person." Rabbi Solomon Ganzfried has emphasized that according to the Jewish law of the Torah, it is forbidden to inflict pain on any living creature.

The great leader of Judaism, Maimonides wrote that, "There is no difference between the pain of man and the pain of other living beings . . . the tenderness of the mother (bird) for her young ones is not produced by reasoning but by feeling, and this faculty exists not only in man but in most living things."

The Christian saint John Chrysostom (AD 347–407) concluded that we ought to show animals "great kindness and gentleness for many reasons, but above all because they are of the same origin as ourselves."

Pope John Paul II has insisted that "It is necessary and urgent that, following the example of the poor man (St. Francis of Assisi), one decides to abandon inconsiderate forms of domination, capture and custody with respect to all creatures." Other contemporary leaders of Christianity have made similar statements, urging for greater respect of God's creatures:

> Cruelty to animals is as if man did not love God.
>
> —Cardinal John Henry Newman

> The earth was made by God and it belongs to God—the churches should reiterate that man is not the real owner of anything, that he is here only as a steward and that he will be judged by the way he treats what has been loaned him.
>
> —Right Rev. Robert Hatch

> Every being has its own interior, its self, its mystery, its numinous aspect. To deprive any being of this sacred quality is to disrupt the total order of the universe. Reverence will be total or it will not be at all.
>
> —Rev. Thomas Berry

Dr. Albert Schweitzer, one of the most outstanding humanitarians of this century concluded:

> To the truly ethical man, all of life is sacred, including forms of life that, from the human point of view, may seem lower than ours.

Islam. The Koran, the holy text of Islam, proclaims, "There is not an animal on earth, nor a flying creature on two wings, but they are like unto you." And the holy prophet of Islam, Muhammad said, "Whoever is kind to the creatures of God is kind to himself."

Hinduism. Hindu religion's text called the *Bhagavad Gita* declares "We bow to all beings with great reverence in the thought that God enters into them through fractioning Himself as living creatures." The great Hindu politician Mahatma Gandhi once said, "The greatness of a nation and its moral progress can be measured by the way in which its animals are treated." Hindu swami Vivekananda advised that, "If you can think of them (animals) as brothers, you have made a little headway towards the brotherhood of all souls, not to speak of the brotherhood of man!"

Jainism. In the Jain religion of India, it is written in the Acaranga Sutra that, "All beings with two, three, four, or five senses . . . in fact all creation, know individually pleasure and displeasure, pain, terror, and sorrow. . . . He who harms animals has not understood or renounced deeds of sin."

Buddhism. Gautama Buddha, who founded the religion of Buddhism observed, "All things are born of the unborn, and from this unity of life flows brotherhood and compassion for all creatures," and that, "The key to a new civilization is the spirit of maitri, friendliness toward all living things." D. T. Suzuki, a world renowned teacher of Buddhism states:

"Buddhists must strive to teach respect and compassion for all creation—compassion is the foundation of their religion."

Finally, we should not forget the wise teachings of the great American Indian chiefs. Black Elk said:

> We should understand well that all things are the works of the Great Spirit. We should know that He is within all things: the trees, the grasses, the rivers, the mountains, all of the four-legged animals, and the winged peoples; and even more important we should understand that He is also above all these things and peoples. When we understand all of this deeply in our hearts, then we will fear, and love, and know the Great Spirit and then we will be and act and live as He intends.

And Chief Seattle (see his letter to President Franklin Pierce on page 167) stated:

> This we know—the earth does not belong to man, man belongs to the earth. All things are connected like the blood that unites one family. Whatever befalls the earth befalls the sons of the earth. Man did not weave the web of life; he is merely a strand of it. Whatever he does to the web, he does to himself.

Even those who don't believe in God recognize that having compassion and humility are two of the highest human virtues. Since compassion is a boundless ethic to be extended to embrace all living things that can suffer or be harmed, it is clearly wrong to treat others—be they human or nonhuman, without compassion and respect.

Abraham Lincoln, the great statesman and President of the United States said "I care not much for a man's religion whose dog and cat are not the better for it." He not only fought against slavery and supported equal rights for all people. He also felt that animals have rights, too stating that "I am in favor of animal rights as well as human rights. That is the way of a whole human being."

Another way to help animals therefore would be to amend the Constitution, as was done when human slavery* was abolished. The following draft of such a revolutionary initiative will generate some lively discussion at home and at school. If such an amendment were ever to be made, what would it mean for the hunter, the butcher, and the zookeeper, among others, as well as the nation's economy?

▪ CONSTITUTIONAL RIGHTS FOR ANIMALS ▪

Whereas animals have a biological kinship with humans since *Homo sapiens* is a species of animal,

And whereas nonhuman animals are part of the same Earth Creation and world-ecological community as we,

And whereas nonhuman animals, including those that have been domesticated or genetically altered, have a will to live, and interests, and a life of their own,

And whereas many nonhuman animal species have basic emotions and needs comparable to those that we possess and experience,

And whereas it is a matter of human dignity and progress as a nation to treat nonhuman animals with respect and compassion,

---

*The Thirteenth Amendment to the US Constitution that abolished slavery states:

Sec. 1: Neither slavery nor involuntary servitude, except as a punishment for crime whereof the party shall have been duly convicted, shall exist within the United States, or any place subject to their jurisdiction.

Sec. 2: Congress shall have power to enforce this article by appropriate legislation.

And whereas it is contrary to the ethics and morality of a civilized society to exclude by omission or commission the rights and interests of all members of the world-ecological community from equal and fair consideration,

So let it be resolved that the Constitution of the United States shall be so amended to read:

1. All nonhuman animals (including all invertebrate species) shall be given the right to equal and fair consideration, since none were made for man's own exclusive use and are "ours" only in sacred trust.
2. Neither cruel exploitation nor subjugation or unnecessary incarceration of nonhuman animals shall exist within the United States or any place subject to their jurisdiction.
3. Nonhuman animals have fundamental interests that shall be weighed against competing human interests, since humans have no absolute right to place their own interests over those of fellow animals.

In the Spring of 1988 thousands of New Jersey high school students became involved in discussing the Constitution of the United States and what amendments they felt were needed. Many students firmly believed that animals should be included and I helped them draft the above rationale and amendment.

It is a noteworthy coincidence that around this same time a papal encyclical on *Social Concerns* was issued by the Vatican. His Holiness Pope John Paul II, in this encyclical "exhorts us to acquire a growing awareness of the fact that one cannot use with impunity the different categories of beings whether living or inanimate—animals, plants, the natural elements—simply as one wishes, according to one's economic needs. On the contrary, one must take into account the nature of each being and of its mutual connection in an ordered system, which is precisely the cosmos."

We might all reflect on the words of Albert Schweitzer who advised us that "Until he extends the circle of compassion to all living things, man himself will not find peace."

The Animal Legal Defense Fund, which includes a network of over 200 attorneys committed to protecting the rights of animals in the US, recently drafted the following model *Animal Bill of Rights*. (For more information you can write to P.O. Box 96041 Washington, D.C. 20077).

Animal Bill of Rights

A petition to the 101st United States Congress

I, the undersigned American Citizen, believe that animals, like all sentient beings, are entitled to basic legal rights in our society. Deprived of legal protection, animals are defenseless against exploitation and abuse by humans. As no such rights now exist, I urge you to pass legislation in support of the following basic rights for animals:

❧ *THE RIGHT of animals to be free from exploitati*
cruelty, neglect and abuse.

❧ *THE RIGHT of laboratory animals not to be used in c.*
or unnecessary experiments.

❧ *THE RIGHT of farm animals to an environment that satisfies their basic physical and psychological needs.*

❧ *THE RIGHT of companion animals to a healthy diet, protective shelter, and adequate medical care.*

❧ *THE RIGHT of wildlife to a natural habitat, ecologically sufficient to a normal existence and a self-sustaining species population.*

❧ *THE RIGHT of animals to have their interests represented in court and safeguarded by the law of the land.*

Signature of petitioner ______________________________

address ______________________________

____

____

____

____

CHAPTER 10

For Parents and Teachers

When I was a child, my parents encouraged my interest in animals, allowing me to collect all kinds of creatures and keep them in jars and cages in my room. I would play for hours along hedge-rows, ditches, ponds and in the fields near my home collecting, identifying, and observing bugs, newts, toads, caterpillars, and such.

My parents and relatives gave me books that enabled me to recognize various kinds of birds and the occasional wild mammal, and the more I read, the more I learned about the ways of nature's creatures. There was usually a dog in the house too, either a neighbor's who had come by to spend the day with me, or a stray that I was allowed to adopt. Going exploring in the fields and woods was even better with a dog I learned, since a good dog will help you find all kinds of interesting things! By the age of ten, I picked up the hobby of collecting bird's eggs from my playmates. This entailed locating a nest, climbing the tree, and taking one egg, usually carried safely in one's mouth during the descent. It didn't take me long to realize that this was unfair to the wildlife, especially since many of the kids in the neighborhood were out stealing eggs, which meant that some nests were quickly cleaned out or abandoned by the parent birds.

In grade school, especially during the springtime, the teacher would set up jars of beans, cress, and pussy willow that we could watch sprout, and there were usually several jars of water bugs and frog-spawn. A small aquarium was stocked with interesting creatures we caught in ponds and in the local canal—stickleback fish, tadpoles, newts, whirligig beetles, dragonflies and caddis fly larvae.

Schools today have these and more—vivariums of ants, earth worms, salamanders; cages or aquarium tanks of rabbits, mice, gerbils, and such. Even if children don't have creatures at home, they will often be exposed to them either at school or at a friend's home. It is easy, however, for children to collect creatures just for the sake of collecting, like stamps or coins. Teachers, and especially parents, should be alerted to this. As a child I once collected over seventy giant elephant hawk moth catterpillars and tried to raise them all at home. Most of them died. Collecting wild creatures should only be encouraged if the child is to learn something about the animals. Excessive collecting should be avoided, and most creatures should be returned to where they were first found after a short period of observation.

Cage and aquarium pets—fish, hamsters, mice, guinea pigs, and the like—require constant attention: regular cleaning, feeding, and watering. No child should simply be allowed to enjoy playing with cage pets and not being responsible for their daily care, otherwise the animals may become nothing more than animated toys.

A dog is the ultimate pet for an older child of nine to twelve years of age. The dog's needs for exercise, grooming, basic obedience training, as well as food, water, and regular health care should be by and large met by the child. An irresponsible child might otherwise grow up to be an irresponsible pet owner and even an irresponsible parent. No child who owns a dog, or any other pet for that matter, should be allowed to get out of caring for it properly and regularly. If the parents show little or no interest in the pet and in the child's care of the pet and relationship with it, the child may soon lose interest. Caring for it then becomes a chore, not a responsibility motivated by affection and respect for the animal's needs. The interest that my parents gave to me, and my involvement in caring for my pets and my wild menagerie of collected creatures, meant that the whole family had a common ground of experiencing and sharing. The crises of a sick or lost dog, a dead hamster, or a neighboring farmer's complaint over one of my strays chasing his cattle, brought us even closer together. Had my parents not been so encouraging and involved, such crises could have divided the family—me and my pet versus them: complaining or insensitive grown-ups, parents, neighbors, and all.

One time when one of my dogs had to be put to sleep I remember coming home to be greeted by one of my aunts who was visiting for the weekend. I told her Rover had been put to sleep. She knew the dog well, but all she said was "Never mind, you'll soon get over it." Such an unfeeling remark to an eight-year-old took many years for me to understand and forgive.* Parents and adults in general don't always realize how much a child (or an adult!) can feel for a pet. Trying to protect oneself from the emotional burden of sharing a child's grief by making light of it is demeaning and potentially harmful.

Feelings are easily brushed aside or misunderstood and a child is quick to pick up adult indifference and insensitivity. Parents can have a profound influence on the emotional de-

* My teacher-consultant Iris Rainone gave me additional insights in this area from one of her seventh-grade student's English-class essays. The student wrote: "One thing that really bugs me is that when an animal dies, most people just say, 'Oh, it was just an animal,' or 'Oh, that's just nature's way of keeping the animal population down.' (When an animal was hit by a car or poisoned, that was not nature). A few days ago my pet mouse died. Milly had lived almost two-and-a-half years . . . at least I spent her last hour with her. My parents said, 'Oh, she's just a mouse.' My mother made me wash my hands. Boy."

velopment of their children. Sharing feelings—grief, joy, anger, and frustration is an important part of growing up. A pet can broaden and deepen the range of emotions that are experienced and expressed within the family. This aspect of pet ownership is not widely recognized. It is certainly of inestimable value, far more than a child simply learning to be responsible for the pet.

The triangle between parents, children, and pets entails even more than responsible care, parental interest, and sharing of feelings and experiences. The other, often neglected question of values and attitudes towards the pet, and animals in general, that the parents have (and which the child acquires from them and from others) are particularly important. Through the ways that the parents instruct, encourage, and intervene (when necessary) with the child's interactions with the pet, the child may or may not acquire any or all of the following: patience, understanding, empathy, compassion. In a word, humaneness.

Many children feel unloved by their parents at times after being disciplined or following an argument or jealous spat with a sibling. A pet may be an invaluable emotional support at such times for the hurt child, especially an all-accepting dog who never judges or loves conditionally. Animals can teach us all the nature and virtue of unconditional love.

Parents who are authoritarian or who hit their children should not be surprised when they see their child ordering the pet around or beating it. Children use parents, other adults, and older peers as role models, and so they tend to mirror the attitudes and values of others in their actions and relationships. Whenever a child abuses a pet, parents should neither scold, ignore or excuse the child, but rather try to find out why the child acted that way.

I received a very sad and disturbing letter from my syndicated newspaper column "Ask Your Vet." It was from a young girl who was desperate over the fact that her father frequently beat the dog with a chain. She had no one to turn to: even her mother seemed to turn a blind eye to the problem. Generally, when someone, adult or child, abuses an animal, that person is emotionally disturbed. A dog is often the scapegoat for inner frustrations and when it does misbehave, it may unleash a tirade of repressed anger. Any child who repeatedly abuses animals should be given psychiatric or psychological counseling, since such abuse is a symptom, not of inborn viciousness, but of some unresolved emotional problem.

Children who are abused by their parents may redirect their aggression onto the nearest, nonthreatening inferior—either a younger sibling or a pet. Many adults with criminal records and sociopathic traits have a childhood history of abusing animals and of parental abuse. There is also a recognized complex of fire-setting, bed-wetting and cruelty to animals in emotionally disturbed children.

Then there is the child who is what I call the "curious scientist." On the surface, the child may seem sadistic, delighting in cutting up worms, poking the cat, and pulling the wings off flies and butterflies. Such behavior is more often motivated by curiosity, a quasi-scientific "what will it do if I do this or that." Parents should not inhibit such natural curiosity but rather instruct the child to simply observe and to respect the animal's right to life. When my daughter, Camilla, was seven, she interceded between a few ants and one of her peers who was squashing them under her feet. "How would you like to be treated like that if you were an ant?" she protested. Questions like this can help a child learn to empathize and to feel compassion, an essential part of being fully human. Children who persist in killing or mutilating animals may be learning such behavior from parents or others who indiscriminately and unthinkingly kill any creature that crawls or flies into the house. Parents who behave in such a way can hardly expect a child to learn respect for all creatures great and small.

I have often wondered why young children, as though by instinct, will often squash an insect under their feet or swat at one with a book. They may be doing more than simply mimicking how adults only too often behave toward usually harmless insects. By such an act of killing they may help assuage their own feelings of vulnerability, smallness, and helplessness by experiencing a false sense of omnipotent power. A humane alternative for parents to teach children would be to gently catch an insect that has found its way into the house and set it free outdoors! I know of some people who, as children, spontaneously acted in this way and who would attempt to rescue drowning insects and worms from puddles and the bathroom sink, and their parents thought that they were odd. Yet compassion toward all creatures is a mark of saintliness, not of insanity or projected insecurity and helplessness. Consider Rishi, the eighteenth-century Japanese monk who would roll up one sleeve while he worked in the fields, so the mosquitos could have their food while he harvested his. He covered his face with a fine net, otherwise he might accidentally kill one of the insects if it landed on his face!

Some children who treat other living creatures as though they are inanimate toys, but who show no malice or redirected aggression in their behavior, may be suffering from infantile autism, a severe form of emotional withdrawal from life. Such children may treat animals as though they are unfeeling machines, such lack of empathy being related to the autistic child's lack of affect.

I recently received a letter from a mother of two children who hated animals and felt that she should not get a cat or a dog for her children even though they wanted one. My advice was for her to seek professional help so that she might overcome her intense dislike of animals. Such fear of animals, termed zoophobia, could be related to an earlier unpleasant experience and if it were not cured, her children would most likely not benefit fully from having a pet. They might even acquire her fear or prejudice.

I feel that it is important for all children to have a pet, for the many reasons outlined above. In the previous case, the parent should not allow her own phobia to limit the oppor-

Fig. 40. Growing up with an affectionate, well-adjusted dog (or cat), like this happy pooch (note the grin of delight) can do much to enrich the life of any child. Photo from Bonnie Smith H.S.U.S.

tunities and experiences of her children. In fact, having a pet could even make her a healthier and better adjusted person.

I recall another sad letter from a young girl whose parents were insisting that she get rid of her guinea pig after the girl had a mild bout of pneumonia. The guinea pig was wrongly seen as a cause of the child's illness.

The negative beliefs, values, and attitudes of parents and teachers toward animals can cause much confusion and distress among children in the family. A prevalent zoophobia is that all animals are dirty and can make one sick. Another is that animals are dangerous. Nothing annoys me more than the parent who tells a child not to go near dogs because they will bite. I had one experience where a four-year-old came up to pet my pooch, who was on the leash and wagging his tail and grinning at the child. I said it was OK to pet the dog but the parent pulled the child away in fear. The happy child looked at the dog and began to scream, the parent's fear and prejudice having been effectively transferred.

A few days later I met a little boy in the park who was about three years old, and afraid of dogs. Fear is not, of course, always learned from the parents. This little boy had been recently knocked over and frightened by a large, playful dog. His father was now desensitizing him by having him watch the dogs playing in the park. Knowing my dog was quiet and friendly, he had his son pet Benji and the transformation was incredible. The little boy's face suddenly lit up. It would not be long before his phobia would be overcome.

I have already stated that a child, provided with the proper parental guidance with a pet, can learn to respect the rights of others and develop empathy and compassion. Since the pet is usually incorporated into the complex network of relationships within the family, parents should also be aware of how and when conflicts between one child and others in the family affect the relationship between the child and pet. Teasing or abusing the pet, as emphasized earlier, may be a symptom of unresolved conflict, not between pet and child, but between the child and some other person.

Having to care for a pet teaches the child more than mere responsibility. Parenting functions may be fostered which will help the child be a more effective and understanding parent later in life. Seeing the need to discipline and train a pet and not spoil it by allowing it to always have its own way, can be one of the most significant learning experiences for children. They are more likely then, to understand that their parents also discipline and instruct them for their own good too.

With this concept in mind, it is a good idea for parents to spend time with, and encourage an older child to work with the family dog and take it through basic obedience classes. The child will learn not only that going to school, even for a dog, is of inestimable value in developing potential, it will also encourage the development of an often-neglected childhood need: self-competence. A child who can instruct and control a dog will acquire considerable self-competence or self-confidence, which is an asset to many shy and insecure children. But this does not entail the child bossing the dog around and becoming a bullying authoritarian. The essence here is that with the right parental attitudes and guidance, a pet can help the child mature and acquire a healthy regard for others in its relationships with both animals and people.

Parental attitudes toward animals are not simply restricted to the relationships with the family pet. Many families that don't have pets, like those with pets, have many occasions when a child will directly or indirectly come across animals, and parental interventions, comments, and reactions can have a significant effect on the child's development of humane and rational values.

For example, how do you react to various animals that you meet or see at the park, zoo, or circus? Your reactions, which reflect your feelings and attitudes, will be picked up

Fig. 41. Parents and teachers can do much to foster humane values in children. Photo from H.S.U.S.

by your children, for better or for worse. At the zoo, do you tell them how savage and mean wolves are, how lions are proud, monkeys dirty and over-sexed, and giraffes ungainly? Or rather than perpetuating such erroneous myths, do you teach the child wrongly to judge animals solely on how they look—beautiful, ugly, cuddly, or loathesome? Do you say nothing when you see a performer at the circus making wild animals do tricks, or when you see a rodeo performer treating steers, calves, and broncos roughly? Do you clarify certain children's stories and old folk tales like Red Riding Hood, that either inaccurately anthropomorphize an animal or endow it with certain attributes that are quite wrong and prejudicial to a true understanding of the nature of animals? Do you encourage your child to hunt and trap wild animals or use live animals in high school science fair projects without exploring the values and justifications, if they exist, behind such activities?

Because we are so civilized in many ways we, and our children, are less and less in touch with nature and with animals both wild and tame. This lack of connection to nature underlies what I call "civilized ignorance"—a growing lack of understanding and appreciation for nature and for all animals wild and tame.

The future of the natural world, of endangered species, and our pets and other domestic animals kept on farms and in research laboratories, lies in part in the hands of parents. If we can inculcate the right attitudes that I have outlined in this chapter, our children and future generations alike may have a greater regard for all life. They might gain a nondiscriminating reverence for all life, which would benefit not only our animal kin, but also improve the quality of relationships between our own kind: compassion rather than exploitation; empathy rather than indifference, and affection rather than conditional love. Living with, and growing up with animals can make us all a little more human, and by that I mean more humane and in touch with others: those animals and humans that give significance and joy to life.

▪ The Animal as Teacher (or Learning Catalyst)

There are innumerable effective learning experiences that a teacher can develop for classroom use, with a dog or other suitable animal as a focus and *catalyst*. This will facilitate student motivation since most children like animals, but not all enjoy seemingly nonrelevant or isolated curriculum areas.

The animal focus could be a highly effective catalyst for reading, creative writing, art, math, history, music and dance, health and nutrition, social studies, etc. As far as curriculum integration is concerned, expansion from the focal animal topic (within the domain of biology or natural history) can be easily accomplished. It is not so much a question of "animalizing" the classroom, but rather of using whatever materials and techniques are available to potentiate learning and motivation: animals, in the right contexts, can be a teacher's best ally, especially in the younger grades. As children mature, their interests tend to become more and more peer-oriented. If their natural interest and curiosity of animals has not been reinforced earlier, they will be difficult to reach via the animal route at the later age. Humane values may, therefore, be harder to instill and indeed there may well be a *critical period* (akin to the critical period for socialization) between five and seven or eight years of age at which time the child is most open and receptive. If animals are not incorporated into the child's socialized sphere of interaction and relatedness in an ambience of humane concern and ethical responsibility during this critical period, there may be less receptivity at a later age. This could also have significant effects on peer relationships since, as we discussed earlier, there is a recognized correlation between antisocial and sociopathic behavior in adults with indifference and cruelty towards animals earlier in life.

Animals can be extremely valuable catalysts* in the classroom not only for the acquisition of cognitive skills but also for developing social/affective skills as well.

---

* There are even more profound and dramatic effects of animal catalysts. For example, their use as therapists has been known to be a positive factor in situations with emotionally-disturbed children and adults, chronic invalids of all ages, and senior citizens in retirement homes.

▪ Examples of Learning Experiences

1. *Emotions and Expressions*
Observe the dog's behavior and body language in various contexts. Compare with man and note similarities in some expressions and therefore in emotions or feelings. Knowing that animals may feel like we do, and have similar needs and emotions—pain, fear, anxiety, pleasure, joy, playfulness, sadness, depression, jealousy, and guilt—how does this influence our responsibilities towards them. (See W. Gates and M. W. Fox. *Superdog: Raising the Perfect Canine Companion*, New York: Howell Books, 1990.)

Fig. 42. A dog in the classroom, with the right teacher or humane society educator, can open many doors as a learning catalyst. Photo: *News Sentinel*, Fort Wayne, IN.

2. *Training (Education)*
Young children should respond and identify well with the fact that a puppy, like a child, has to learn things for its own good and for the well-being of others, whose rights and needs must be respected. Ways to housebreak (toilet train) and how to teach the dog to come, sit, stay, and behave on the leash (especially near traffic) can be learned and appreciated by the child. Such role-reversal—the child as teacher—can be a valuable learning experience in itself.

3. *General Care*
How to care for the pet—the right shelter, food, water, exercise, veterinary treatment (shots), regular grooming, etc., relate to self-care and to more general principles of health, hygiene, and nutrition. Children often take on a parental role with their pets, which may be extremely valuable for instilling responsible care and understanding for later parenthood. The way that animals take care of themselves can also be instructive. We can learn a lot by observing their habits ranging from self-grooming to self-preservation.

Also, how animals care for each other—as a mother dog will nurse, groom, and clean her pups, regurgitate food for them and even defend them from strangers—can be described, observed at a kennel, or shown in suitable films or slides.

Other Related Topics: Expanding Awareness

Expansion into other curriculum areas can also be accomplished using a dog as a focus and catalyst.

a) *History*. The various uses of the dog in human history up to the present day, demonstrating how some animals are a human's best friend (but is the reverse always true?)

b) *Literature and Creative Writing*. There are several classic short and long stories about dogs, and of course, any child in the class who has a dog at home may be easily motivated to write about some particular experience with the pet.

c) *Social Studies*. The various roles of the dog in society and the problems of pet overpopulation, need for birth control, etc., lend themselves to topics for curriculum expansion.

d) *Science and Mathematics*. Experiments involving any *direct* treatment of any animal (surgery, injecting drugs, experimental diets, etc.) should be outlawed in schools. Students can become competent scientists by developing their latent observational abilities. (Unfortunately, trivial manual dexterity such as giving injections or doing dissections and learning other mechanical skills seem to be the major goal of most science fair projects involving animal studies). What students observe can be recorded, and their analytical skills developed through quantitative analysis of qualitative data, such as how often a male dog marks trees and other objects when he goes for a walk; which objects are preferred, when and why does he scrape the ground with his feet after marking, etc.* Mathematical questions can cover a range of topics such as calculating how many relatives a female dog could leave when it breeds once a year for six years, has three female pups each litter, and each of which has the same reproductive potential as the mother!

---

* See Allen W. Stokes, *Animal Behavior in Laboratory and Field*, W. H. Freeman & Co. and M. W. Fox, *Understanding Your Dog*, *Understanding Your Pet*, and *Understanding Your Cat* (New York: Coward McCann), for more topics for use with older students.

Humane Education: Some Thoughts and Formulations

Inculcating humane values alone should not be the goal of the humane-oriented educator. Rather, it should be realized that humaneness is a key to be used to liberate people of all ages from an egocentric/humanocentric regard for others into a new state of awareness that comprises both compassionate and empathetic concern for all life and responsible ethical constraints in relation to the intrinsic rights of others.

A teacher, who, for example, is in a school where the childrens' parents operate a livestock or poultry factory farm or hunt and trap animals may feel intimidated and may be threatened or dismissed if he or she imposes his or her (humane or sentimental) values upon the children. Even class textbooks and most childrens' books try to avoid creating any controversies. It is little wonder that children become bored with such unstimulating tasteless pablum. Their minds are best developed when they explore controversies and their values as the friction of opposing views sparks classroom debate. Teachers need not *impose* their own values (and risk being branded by parents and others) but instead, carefully evaluate consensus values by having the children explore and discuss their own and others' actions and values. The Socratic method here should prove extremely effective once the discussion turns to focus upon ethical issues and dilemmas (must we kill to live?) and ultimately upon the intrinsic rights of other living things and the nature of our relationship and responsibilities towards others.

CHAPTER 11

People and Animals—Ethical Concerns: A Personal View

As a veterinarian, ethologist, and concerned humanitarian, I am not in favor of people keeping animals as pets unless they know how to feed and care for them properly. Pet owners should provide their pets with veterinary care when needed, and as a routine, for preventive purposes. I favor people adopting cats and dogs, or kittens and puppies, from animal shelters. The deliberate breeding of cats and dogs, especially purebred ones that suffer from an ever increasing number of genetic defects, is unethical and self-indulgent when so many unwanted cats and dogs are being abandoned, the majority of which must finally be euthanized.

I am in favor of knowledgeable people keeping various native species of orphaned and injured wildlife that cannot be set free, rather than keeping wild animals that have been deliberately caught, bred, or imported for sale as pets.

I am in favor of vegetarianism (and organic farming) because of the inherent suffering and sickness of animals raised on factory farms. These factory farms have contributed to the demise of smaller family farms. They reduce the diversity and ecological stability of agriculture. They also jeopardize consumer health (because of the many drugs used to control disease and to boost productivity). Furthermore, they endanger wildlife by reducing natural populations and pushing many species toward extinction because land is taken over (and often contaminated with pesticides) to raise feed for farm animals. Modern animal agriculture is an inefficient practice, and a waste of nonrenewable resources. Hence I am in favor of a humane sustainable agriculture and encourage meat-eaters to support farmers who have adopted humane, sustainable husbandry practices.

I am in favor of the phasing out of all experiments on animals for human medical and other commercial/industrial purposes. Medical science has reached the stage where continued emphasis upon animal research and testing may actually inhibit medical progress since, for ideological, political, and economic reasons, insufficient attention is given to preventive, environmental, and behavioral medicine. I consider it unethical for students to make animals suffer as part of their education. They should learn from the already sick and injured, as should graduate researchers in veterinary, human medical, and other sciences, notably psychology.

I am in favor of the kind of stewardship of wildlife and of endangered species in captivity that is aimed at the protection and restoration of natural ecosystems rather than their management primarily for commercial and recreational purposes, notably monoculture forestry, hunting, and trapping.

I am in favor of the development of appropriate technologies, industries and food-production systems consonant with the principle of humane planetary stewardship. These technologies recognize the rights of all living things to a whole and healthy environment and the rights of each living thing to equal and fair consideration.

Animals need to be liberated from all forms of human domination and exploitation, from the doping of horses and dog fighting, to vivisection and hunting. Animals are not commodities, nor were they created for our own use and unjust dominion, rather they are entrusted to us and we demean our own humanity when we fail to give them equal and fair consideration. Humility and compassionate reverence for all life are essential aspects of a wise and enlightened planetary stewardship, for if we do not stop the poisoning and destruction of nature and the holocaust of the animal kingdom and show reverence to all life, no matter what economic or other justification we may have to the contrary, their fate will be ours also.

Appendix I

▪ Toward a More Humane and Ecologically Harmonizing Life-Style:*

The Food We Eat

Modern intensive farming systems are inhumane, especially for veal calves and to a slightly lesser extent for pigs, poultry, and egg-laying hens. Eat no veal or calf liver, and eat no beef, pork, bacon, chicken, and eggs (unless these products are guaranteed to come from humanely-raised animals, like free-range eggs and 'natural' range beef). Then there will be less suffering. Balance your diet and improve your health with high protein vegetables—lentils, beans, tofu—and more fresh vegetables, grains, and fruits that are in season. Cheese, yogurt, and other dairy products are generally acceptable if you can find dairy farmers whose cows are not kept under inhumane, intensive conditions.

Avoid tuna until the fishing industry does more to reduce the destruction of dolphins. Eat no imported goose liver (paté de fois gras) or turtle; geese are unhumanely force-fed and turtles are becoming endangered through overharvesting.

---

* From M. W. Fox, *Understanding Your Pet,* (NY: Coward, McCann, 1978).

These dietary decisions are personal of course, and vegetarianism is too difficult for some. I would advocate nonvegetarians to at least become "conscientious omnivores," aware of what they eat.

The Products We Consume

Stick to old (tried, true, and tested) brands, especially of toiletries, household cleaning agents, and nonprescription drugs (particularly eye and mouth washes). New and improved products and products developed to corner the consumer market with novel, but nonessential innovation, involve countless animal lives, and often unjustifiable pain and suffering in the course of running safety tests for the consumer. Sticking to the old brands will help reduce industry's incentive to use and abuse more animals in researching and developing more new nonessential products. As more companies recognize what more and more people want to know, look out for products that say "not animal tested" on the label.

Perfumes should contain no musk (from wild civet cats and other mammals) or ambergris (from whales). Cosmetics labeled as being of vegetable origin will not contain the oil of turtle, or whale, or other animal extracts, which the label on the bottle will not usually disclose. Also watch out for whale-oil lubricants and mink-oil products.

Clothes and Objects

The smaller your wardrobe, the less energy you will consume: cotton and wool are more economical than synthetic (polyester) materials. Kapok and other synthetic fibers are more humane insulators of parkas than duck and goose down. Wear no wild animal furs, even if the animal is not on the endangered species list; these are inhumanely caught and their use for personal decoration alone is ethically untenable. On the basis of this latter point, all ranch-raised furs should be avoided also. Heavy cotton sweaters and Kapok-filled jackets and parkas will keep you just as warm!

Art objects and personal accoutrements may be made from wild animal products—avoid them, since to purchase such objects is to support the needless killing of animals. Avoid art objects and other things made from butterflies, bird's feathers, snake and other animal skins, alligator and ostrich products, sealskin, elephant and walrus ivory, and tortoiseshell (statues, chess sets, jewelry, etc.). Alternative materials are abundant and attractive.

The Shows and Sports We Enjoy

Be on the lookout for TV shows and films, adult and children's books that abuse or demean our animal kin. Voice complaints to the TV networks and their sponsors, local movie houses, bookstores, and public and school libraries. Media materials that create or perpetuate false or negative myths and attitudes toward animals and that detract from the humane ethic of animal rights should be protested against and boycotted. Dog- and cock-fight entertainment, greased-pig catching, bullfights, raccoon baiting, and fox hunting are inhumane and should be boycotted and protested. Also, because conditions are such that animal abuses are frequent and often unavoidable, horse racing and greyhound racing (which in many states involves prior training with live rabbits and cats) are ethically unacceptable. Other sports, including trophy- and big-game hunting, hunting with bow and arrow, and trophy (deep-sea) fishing, are to be condemned. Hunting as a nonsubsistence activity is ethically and ecologically untenable. Roadside zoos, some municipal zoos, and circuses with various animal acts demand rigorous scrutiny. Alternatives and substitutes are many: soccer, baseball and football for the spectator; nature photography and natural-history study for the hunter/killer; and roulette or backgammon for the horse-race gambler are just a few!

House and Garden

Avoid using nonselective pesticides and herbicides; they kill indiscriminately, innocent creatures as well as pests and weeds, and they may kill or harm you or your children. Turning lights off on the patio will keep bugs away, as will personal bug repellents. Don't use bug sprays or electric bug zappers: only a few of the millions you kill would have bitten you and some insects are useful or necessary in the many natural cycles. If you have a big lawn, let some part go to seed and create a meadow for butterflies and other insects, and for birds and reptiles. This way, you will provide (at no cost!) seeds for the birds and small rodents during the winter. The more energy you can conserve, the fewer goods you buy, and the less meat you use, the more energy there will be available for the rest of the world and less damage will be done to areas where the wildlife is threatened by strip-mining, oil spills, deforestation, hydro-electric dam construction, and pollution.

The Animals We Enjoy

Before you obtain a pet—be it a dog, cat, gerbil, parakeet, or whatever—read about how to care for it first. You may discover that your life-style is not compatible with keeping a dog, or your home might not be right for a new cat or other pet.

As far as wild creatures are concerned, do not purchase them in a pet store or anywhere! Even those that have been imported or raised in captivity. To sell wild animals as pets is a gross misrepresentation (I think it should be labeled fraud). Any life form taken from the wild for study or enjoyment should be returned as soon as possible to the same place, and in the same condition in which it was found (or better).

Unfortunately, it is a long time, as I see it, before humans will cease to exploit, manipulate, and control wild or domestic animals, other people, or pristine wilderness and ocean. The weakness of humanity is a blindness, which some call ignorance, where a selfish and immature ego claims the world as its own and prevents it from seeing itself as a part of the world. Kinship with all life is a biological, evolutionary fact. Unfortunately our consumptive culture, our ways of doing, perceiving, and relating, blind us to this reality, and to the spiritual union of all living things which only we, as stewards of planet earth, can express in an ethic of reverence for all life. A mere shift in the way we see and relate can change the world, because as humanity sees, so they are. A pet animal can catalyze such an awareness, and this book, working through animals, humans, and their interrelationship has, I hope, helped in this direction.

I hope you will begin your first steps along this road immediately after setting this book aside.

Appendix II

The following is the final text, adopted by the International League for Animal Rights and affiliated national leagues on the occasion of the Third International Meeting on the Rights of Animals (London, 21–23 September 1977). The Declaration, proclaimed on 15 October 1978 by the International League, affiliated leagues, associations, and individuals who wish to be associated with it, was submitted to the United Nations Educational, Scientific, and Cultural Organization (U.N.E.S.C.O.), and then to the United Nations Organization (U.N.O.). It was accompanied by a petition signed by over two million people.

▪ UNIVERSAL DECLARATION OF THE ▪ RIGHTS OF ANIMALS

PREAMBLE

Whereas all animals have rights,

Whereas disregard and contempt for the rights of animals have resulted and continue to result in crimes by man against nature and against animals,

Whereas recognition by the human species of the right to existence of other animal species is the foundation of the coexistence of species throughout the animal world,

Whereas genocide has been perpetrated by man on animals and the threat of genocide continues

Whereas respect for animals is linked to the respect of man for men,

Whereas from childhood man should be taught to observe, understand, respect, and love animals,

IT IS HEREBY PROCLAIMED:

Article 1.

All animals are born with an equal claim on life and the same rights to existence.

Article 2.

i. All animals are entitled to respect.

ii. Man as an animal species shall not arrogate to himself the right to exterminate or inhumanely exploit other animals. It is his duty to use his knowledge for the welfare of animals.

iii. All animals have the right to the attention, care and protection of man.

Article 3.

i. No animal shall be ill-treated or be subject to cruel acts.

ii. If an animal has to be killed, this must be instantaneous and without distress.

Article 4.

i. All wild animals have the right to liberty in their natural environment, whether land, air or water, and should be allowed to procreate.

ii. Deprivation of freedom, even for educational purposes, is an infringement of this right.

Article 5.

i. Animals of species living traditionally in a human environment have the right to live and grow at the rhythm and under the conditions of life and freedom peculiar to their species.

ii. Any interference by man with this rhythm or these conditions for purposes of gain is an infringement of this right.

Article 6.

i. All companion animals have the right to complete their natural life span.

ii. Abandonment of an animal is a cruel and degrading act.

Article 7.

All working animals are entitled to a reasonable limitation of the duration and intensity of their work, to the necessary nourishment and to rest.

Article 8.

i. Animal experimentation involving physical or psychological suffering is incompatible with the rights of animals, whether it be for scientific, medical, commercial, or any other form of research.

ii. Replacement methods must be used and developed.

Article 9.

Where animals are used in the food industry they shall be reared, transported, lairaged, and killed without the infliction of suffering.

Article 10.

i. No animal shall be exploited for the amusement of man.

ii. Exhibitions and spectacles involving animals are incompatible with their dignity.

Article 11.

Any act involving the wanton killing of an animal is biocide, that is, a crime against life.

Article 12.

i. Any act involving the mass killing of wild animals is genocide, that is, a crime against the species.

ii. Pollution or destruction of the natural environment leads to genocide.

Article 13.

i. Dead animals shall be treated with respect.

ii. Scenes of violence involving animals shall be banned from cinema and television, except for humane education.

Article 14.

i. Representatives of movements that defend animals' rights should have an effective voice at all levels of government.

ii. The rights of animals, like human rights, should enjoy the protection of law.

London, September 1977

Appendix III

(For Parents and Teachers)

▪ The Genetic Engineering of Animals

Animals are now the subjects of a new form of human exploitation called genetic engineering. Greater public understanding of this will help ensure better protection of these animals in the years to come.

What is genetic engineering? Genetic engineering entails the insertion or "gene splicing" of certain genes from one life-form into another. Examples include inserting the human growth gene into a pig or mouse embryo; the antifreeze gene of flounders into catfish and carp; a virus particle of AIDS disease into the genetic makeup of mice. These genes, which are inserted by a variety of techniques, including microinjection, cell fusion, electroporation, and transformation, contain a hereditary material known as DNA (deoxyribonucleic acid), the substance that regulates the biochemical activities of all living cells. The use of this research enables scientists to create so-called transgenic animals, animals which could not be bred by traditional selection or artificial insemination methods. The consequences can be permanent since in becoming an integral part of the animals' hereditary makeup, they can be passed on to future generations.

What are transgenic animals? They are those animals whose hereditary material, or DNA, has been changed by various so-called genetic engineering techniques. This entails the addition of foreign DNA from a source other than parental germplasm, usually from a different animal species, including the human species.

What animal species have been made transgenic? Most research (there are fewer than 100 laboratories worldwide) has been done on mice and farm animals—pigs, sheep, goats, cattle, chickens, and some fish species of commercial value.

Why are human genes most often chosen to put into animals: This is simply for convenience because they are most readily available, since much research has been done identifying, extracting, and characterizing human genes.

Why is this research being done? To learn more about how genes function; to find cures for human diseases, using genetically engineered animals as models of human genetic and developmental disorders and diseases like diabetes, cancer, and AIDS; to turn animals into protein factories—called molecular farming—so they produce pharmaceutical drugs and biologics in their milk; to make farm animals leaner, to make them grow faster, produce more milk and eggs, and have greater disease resistance.

Isn't genetic engineering simply an extension of traditional animal breeding practices? Traditional breeding practices included selective breeding within species and occasional crossbreeding between very closely related species (offspring often being sterile like a mule, the result of crossbreeding between a horse and donkey). Breeding transgenic animals is of a very different order, because the genes from totally unrelated species are being introduced by techniques that are far from natural and often have unforeseen harmful consequences, causing fetal death, mutations, and various abnormalities.

Other biotechnology techniques are also being used on farm and laboratory animals, notably embryo transfer, cloning, and embryo-fusion to create chimeras like the "geep"—sheep with a goat's head.

Will animals suffer? Veterinary biotechnology, in developing new vaccines and diagnostics, will help advance the overall health and welfare of animals. But increased disease resistance in farm animals won't mean an end to cruel and stressful intensive factory-farming methods, or to the suffering that arises from those methods.

Genetically engineered animals have already been subjected, in the course of research, to both deliberately induced and unanticipated suffering. Hundreds of transgenic mice have suffered and died from various forms of cancer and other genetically created diseases. Transgenic pigs carrying human growth genes suffered from abnormal hormone production and developed gastric ulcers. crippling arthritis, and other skeletal abnormalities and had impaired disease resistance.

Are there environmental concerns? There are many risks with the deliberate release of genetically engineered bacteria, viruses and plant pests and pathogens such as insects and fungi. The risks with agricultural animals are considerable: escape of gene-engineered viruses (including live virus vaccines), their possible mutation and their transmission to humans and other animals; introduction of livestock (and agricultural crops) genetically engineered to be disease-resistant and climate-adapted into cleared wildlife habitats, potentially leading to accelerated extinction of wildlife and decline in global biodiversity. The accidental release of genetically engineered fish could have devastating ecological consequences to both marine and freshwater life.

How can the benefits of genetic engineering be maximized for society as a whole? It is recognized that there are benefits to be derived from genetic engineering research. But, if society is to benefit from this research, ethical, animal welfare, and environmental concerns should not be preempted in exchange for short-term economic gain.

What about genetically-engineered farm-animal produce? Ethical and environmental concerns notwithstanding, the genetic engineering of farm animals is the culmination of six to eight thousand years of increasing control and manipulation via the process of domestication. This process is now being accelerated and intensified by changing the genetic makeup of farm animals, and by altering their structure and physiology by treating them with genetically-engineered products to influence their growth, size, digestive abilities, fertility, lactation, appetites, and disease-resistance under intensive farming conditions. Stressful factory conditions are not, however, being improved. Rather, genetic engineering biotechnology is being applied to boost profits and productivity under existing conditions. From a preventive and holistic veterinary perspective, this is neither sound science, nor good medicine.

On the basis of medically valid concern and scientifically documented evidence*, the health and welfare of farm ani-

* For further documentation of the risks and suffering of animals subjected to genetic-engineering, see M. W. Fox, *Animal Welfare Concerns of Genetic Engineering Biotechnology*, The Humane Society of the United States, Washington, DC, 1988.

mals under present husbandry conditions will be placed in even greater jeopardy by genetic engineering biotechnology. The Humane Society of the United States therefore opposes all such applications of this technology in farm animals until there is sound scientific and veterinary medical evidence to the contrary.

Furthermore, independent of consumer food-safety assurances, any and all products derived from genetically-engineered farm animals and from farm animals treated with genetically-engineered drugs should be appropriately labelled. The right of consumers to know how farm animals, whose products they would consume, have actually been treated, is integral to a just and democratic society. Likewise, their freedom of choice should be recognized and protected by appropriate labeling of animal produce, e.g., hormone-treated; organic; free range; humanely-raised, etc.

How can animals' welfare be better assured? While no technology is risk-free, the appropriate application of biotechnology should strive for the enhancement of the quality of life from a number of perspectives, including environmental and animal welfare considerations. Since genetic-engineering research on animals is unpredictable by nature, experiments have already resulted in animal suffering which can be directly attributed to genetic engineering. The situation is critical because most genetic engineering research is conducted using animals that are either not covered by the Animal Welfare Act (AWA), or will not be protected because enforcement is spotty and superficial for those who are considered covered. In light of these problems the Congress and the U.S. Department of Agriculture (USDA) should address the unique suffering potential in genetic-engineering research. For example, the USDA could enforce its authority to apply the Animal Welfare Act to farm animals used for nonagricultural purposes (i.e., molecular farming). Consideration should be given to amending the AWA to provide protection for mice and other rodent species most widely used in genetic engineering research and development. While the issue of justifying unavoidable animal suffering will continue to be debated and legislatively regulated, the new field of genetic engineering raises many fundamental ethical and environmental concerns and brings with it new ways by which animals may be harmed and caused to suffer. And while no technology is risk-free, what should be considered appropriate application of biotechnology should be the enhancement of the quality of life from an environmental and animal protection perspective, and not from a narrow economic or other human-interest perspective exclusively.

What does the patenting of animals have to do with genetic engineering? The US Patent and Trademark Office ruled that all animals that have been genetically altered by biotechnology, and are thus regarded as unique human inventions, can be patented. Since microorganisms (viruses, bacteria, etc.) and plants that have been genetically-engineered can also be patented, this means that (with the exclusion of human beings) *all life forms can now be patented*, once they have been genetically-engineered. The Humane Society of the United States (HSUS) and many other organizations including conservation and farming associations are opposed to this ruling, and support a congressional moratorium on animal patenting so that the ethical, animal suffering, economic, and environmental consequences of patenting can be thoroughly addressed.

Why should humanitarians be concerned about animal patenting? Society stands to benefit from advances that will be possible through genetic engineering. But, as with many of the world's scientific advances in the past, there are potential consequences that should be addressed early on. These concerns, especially the ethical and animal suffering questions, will be exacerbated by animal patenting because patenting itself will provide an economic impetus that could override ethical and animal welfare concerns if safeguards have not been instituted.

But isn't there room for some hope? With an empathic attitude of respect for life; humility, benevolence, and trust, not in science alone but in the wisdom of working and living in harmony with the Earth's processes, there is hope. Through its appropriate application, biotechnology could indeed help us heal ourselves and the Earth. But first we must have the right attitudes, ethics, and values, as well as appropriate laws and industry regulations that will assure our humane and creative planetary participation.

Appendix IV

▪ Animal Protection Laws

This report was prepared by the Humane Society of the United States in August 1979. It summarizes the major federal legislation and lists sources for information on state and local legislation. Since 1979 some of these laws have been amended slightly but no new animal protection laws have been enacted.

Federal Laws

The name of each act is followed by its congressional number and information on the history of its passage and any amendments which have been made.

THE ANIMAL WELFARE ACT (7 U.S.C. §2131 et seq.; passed 1966, amended 1970 and 1976). The Animal Welfare Act established sweeping regulatory system to protect dogs, cats and many species of wild animals from abuse and represents the direct involvement of the federal government, to the maximum extent of its constitutional power, in the cause of animal welfare. This statute regulates individuals and establishments which buy or sell animals for research or exhibition purposes and to a limited extent the pet trade. Animal dealers, research laboratories, pet stores offering wild animals for sale, animal auctions, zoos, circuses and animal trainers are required by law to provide humane care, treatment and handling for the animals they house. The Act is administered by the U.S. Department of Agriculture (USDA).

The U.S. Department of Agriculture enforces regulations which set minimum husbandry standards for feeding and watering, cage size, sanitation, temperature range, veterinary care and euthanasia. Dealers and most exhibitors are required to be licensed and pay fees based on a sliding schedule. Others such as laboratories are required to register but do not pay fees. Common carriers (airlines, railroads, trucking companies, etc.) must register and adhere to standards developed to assure humane transportation.

Birds, reptiles, rodents, and farm animals are not covered by the Animal Welfare Act. In June 1979 USDA issued regulations covering the care, treatment, and handling of marine mammals in captivity, offering protection to them for the first time.

The 1966 Animal Welfare Act was motivated largely by Congressional concern about the theft of pet animals for sale to research labs. Animals now must be held five days by dealers and exhibitors before sale. Records of purchases or sales and animals on hand must be kept. Both requirements are designed to facilitate the tracing of stolen animals.

Although research laboratories are required to adhere to the USDA standards for humane treatment, in boarding their animals, the actual conduct of any experiment is expressly exempted. Researchers are directed to use appropriate analgesics, anesthetics, tranquilizers and painkillers, but this requirement is automatically lifted if, according to the researcher, the use of one of these substances would interfere with the action of the experiment. The animal care veterinarian of the institution is responsible for the fulfillment of this requirement.

The 1976 amendments included provisions to make animal fighting a federal offense. Animal fighting ventures are illegal under this statute whenever interstate or foreign commerce is involved. This law makes it illegal for anyone to sponsor an animal in any animal fighting venture, to sell, buy, transport or deliver any animal for this purpose and to use the mails to promote an animal fighting venture. All dog fighting is covered under this statute, but cockfighting is only punishable under the Animal Welfare Act in states where it is not legal. Although the USDA, through its Office of Investigations, is immediately responsible for administration of this law, the department may obtain the assistance of the FBI, the Department of the Treasury or other law enforcement agencies on the federal, state, or local levels. Search and seizure warrants can be issued and civil and criminal penalties can be levied against violators.

For violations other than the animal fighting sections, cease and desist orders may be issued against violators and licenses may be suspended. Civil and criminal penalties are another legal recourse against violations of the Act.

Animal and Plant Health Inspection Service (APHIS) has regional inspectors and veterinarians who conduct periodic inspections and investigate any violations. Part-time inspectors and private veterinarians who work on a fee basis also conduct inspections.

The USDA has come under fire for poor enforcement of the Act. Violations have continued without correction or legal action. Strong enforcement has been lacking. Funding has been insufficient and the federal inspectors and veterinarians spend only five per cent of their time on Animal Welfare Act issues. Most of the time, they work on livestock disease eradication. For questions, complaints, or information, write to:

Administrator
Animal and Plant Health Inspection Service
USDA
Washington, D.C. 20250

MARINE MAMMAL PROTECTION ACT OF 1972 (16 U.S.C. §§ 1361–1407; passed 1972, amended 1973 and 1976). In the Marine Mammal Protection Act (MMPA), Congress set forth a national policy to maintain marine mammal populations at optimum sustainable levels (OSP), while maintaining the health and stability of the marine ecosystem. This law established a moratorium of indefinite duration during which no marine mammals could be taken (killed, harassed, etc.) by any person subject to the jurisdiction of the United States. Nor, during the moratorium, can any imports be made of marine mammals or products from them.

Certain exceptions to the moratorium are allowed. The public display industry (marinelands, zoos, etc.) and the scientific community can apply for a permit to obtain marine mammals. Generally, they are granted. Natives in Alaska are also allowed to continue taking marine mammals for subsistence. The tuna fishing industry was given a two-year "grace" period for the purpose of developing technology in order to stop killing porpoises incidentally in the course of fishing. (Two years was not enough and after three more years of court cases and Congressional hearings, the tuna industry is now under a strict regulatory regime forcing them to reduce porpoise mortality and serious injury rate to near zero.)

In addition to the moratorium, the Act bans importation of any marine mammal or product if the animal was taken in an inhumane manner, or if it was nursing, or less than eight months old at the time it was taken. This provision effectively bans import of the Canadian white baby harp seal skins.

A mechanism is available to "waive" the moratorium both for importing and taking marine mammals. If the applicant can prove that the taking is humane, that the stocks are at OSP, and that a management scheme is in place which will maintain the stocks at the OSP level and is consistent with the Act, then a waiver may be granted.

One waiver of the moratorium has been granted to allow walrus to be killed in Alaska. A waiver to allow the import of South African seal skins was voided by the Courts because the seal pups were nursing, and were less than eight months old when killed. Also, the State of Alaska has applied for a waiver for eight of its marine mammal species which would effectively reopen sport hunting of many of these mammals. Their application is pending.

The administration of the MMPA is split between the Department of Commerce (National Marine Fisheries Service) for whales, dolphins, porpoise and seals; and the Department of the Interior (Fish and Wildlife Service) for manatees, dugongs, sea otters, polar bears and walrus.

The Act also created a third arm called the Marine Mammal Commission which is an independent scientific advisory body charged with reviewing policies and actions of the federal agencies and making recommendations to further the objectives of the Act.

Civil and criminal penalties are available under the Act.

A 1978 amendment to the law makes it illegal to conduct commercial whaling in waters subject to the jurisdiction of the U.S.

For any questions, complaints, or information, you can write to the appropriate agency:

Director
National Marine Fisheries Service
U.S. Department of Commerce
Washington, D.C. 20235

Director
Fish and Wildlife Service
Department of the Interior
Washington, D.C. 20240

THE HUMANE METHODS OF SLAUGHTER ACT (7 U.S.C. 1901 et seq., P.L. 95–445; passed 1958, amended 1978). These statutes require that livestock must be stunned by humane methods prior to slaughter. The 1958 law defined these methods as those which render livestock insensible to pain by a single blow or gunshot or electrical or chemical means that are rapid and effective before being shackled, hoisted, thrown, cast, or cut. Slaughter in accordance with the ritual requirements of a religious faith is exempted, provided that the prescribed method causes the animal to suffer loss of consciousness by anemia of the brain caused by the simultaneous and instantaneous severance of the carotoid [*sic*] arteries.

From 1958 until October 1979, when the 1978 law takes effect, only slaughterhouses selling meat to the federal government were covered by the humane law. The U.S. Department of Agriculture administered the law and maintained lists of slaughterhouses stating which plants used humane, non-humane, or ritual methods. It was the responsibility of federal purchasing agents to assure that the meat purchased was from slaughterhouses employing humane methods. Plants not adhering to humane standards were technically ineligible for federal contracts, however, enforcement appears to have been non-existent. No record of a plant being denied a federal contract exists. Nor is it known whether any federal purchasing agent ever checked slaughter methods. The 1958 law will be superceded [*sic*] by the new law (P.L. 95–445) although the same provisions delineating what is a humane method will be incorporated into the new law.

The 1978 Humane Methods of Slaughter Act amended the Federal Meat Inspection Act by incorporating humane slaughter standards into federal meat inspection standards, and making plants violating these standards subject to strong penalties. Administration of the Act remained with the U.S. Department of Agriculture.

As a result of the enactment of the P.L. 95–445, all slaughterhouses engaged in interstate or foreign commerce and all plants in states which do not maintain a separate state meat inspection system for interstate plants, will be monitored for compliance with this law by federal meat inspectors. The inspectors will be able to take a range of actions to prevent the inhumane slaughter of livestock, including "withholding inspection" which is tantamount to closing down plant operations.

Slaughterhouses, which only do business within their own state and are located in states which have separate state meat inspection programs, will eventually have to adopt humane slaughter methods. Integral to the Federal Meat Inspection Act is a requirement that any state meat inspection system's standards are at least equal to the federal. As a result, the states which do not have humane slaughter statutes and are not totally under federal inspection, will have to enact new legislation or issue new regulations. These states are being granted additional time for compliance to allow them to pass new laws.

In addition, the new law will require that foreign slaughterhouses exporting meat to the United States will have to comply with the humane standards just as they currently have to comply with health standards in the Federal Meat Inspection Act.

Also as a result of the 1978 law, federal meat inspectors will check that livestock are being humanely treated from the time that they arrive at the slaughterhouse until slaughter. The Senate Committee Report on the 1978 law stated that preslaughter handling as cited in the original law should be interpreted to begin when the livestock comes into custody of the slaughterhouse. Previously, inspectors had no authority to prevent abuse of the livestock by slaughterhouse personnel. Regulations will be issued defining standards for humane preslaughter handling.

For further information on this statute contact:

Administrator
Food Safety and Quality Service
U.S. Department of Agriculture
Washington, D.C. 20250

THE HORSE PROTECTION ACT (15 U.S.C. §§ 1821 et seq.; passed 1970, amended 1976). This law prohibits exhibition or transportation in commerce for show or exhibition of any horse which has been sored for the purpose of affecting its natural gait. The Act also prohibits the use of chains, boots, and other devices which may reasonably be expected to cause physical pain or distress to a horse. The management of horse shows are required to disqualify any "sored" horse. The United States Department of Agriculture through the regional inspection system of the Animal and Plant Health Inspection Service, enforces this law. The Department also relies on self-policing activities by the industry. Civil and criminal penalties may be levied against offenders. For further information, contact:

Administrator
Animal and Plant Health Inspection Service
USDA
Washington, D.C. 20250

TULE ELK PRESERVATION ACT (P.L. 94–389; passed 1976). This statute directs a Federal/State cooperative program for the preservation and enhancement of Tule Elk, an animal native to California. The Secretary of the Interior is directed to make an annual report to Congress in March of each year on activities carried out under the Act.

BALD EAGLE PROTECTION ACT (16 U.S.C. § 668 et seq.; passed in 1940, amended 1959, 1962, and 1972). This law provides protection for the bald eagle (the national emblem) and the golden eagle by prohibiting except under certain specified conditions, the capture, killing, or possession of and commerce in such birds. The Department of the Interior administers this law.

LACEY ACT (18 U.S.C. § 42–44; passed 1900, amended 1948, 1949, 1960, and 1969). The Lacey Act prohibits importation of wild vertebrates and other animals declared by the Secretary of the Interior to be injurious to man, agriculture, forestry, and wildlife resources except under certain circumstances such as zoological, educational, medical, and scientific purposes. It also prohibits the transportation in interstate or foreign commerce of wildlife or their parts or products taken or possessed in violation of federal, state, or foreign laws or regulations issued pursuant to those laws. The Department of the Interior took over enforcement of this law from the Department of Agriculture in 1939. To date, there has been only uneven enforcement of this law.

For further information on the Lacey Act, Tule Elk Preservation Act, and Bald Eagle Protection Act, write to:

Director
Fish and Wildlife Service
Department of the Interior
Washington, D.C. 20240

EXPORT OF HORSES BY SEA (P.L. 95–52). The Export Administration Amendments of 1977 contain a provision forbidding the export of horses by sea for slaughter. The Department of Commerce is responsible for administering this law.

For further information, contact:

Secretary of Commerce
Commerce Building
14th Street and Constitution Avenue, NW
Washington, D.C. 20230

THE WILD, FREE-ROAMING HORSES AND BURROS ACT (16 U.S.C., §§ 1331–1430 and 95–514; passed 1971, amended 1978). The original 1971 statute protected wild horses and burros on federal lands administered by the Bureau of Land Management (BLM), Department of the Interior and the U.S. Forest Service (USFS), Department of Agriculture. Congress determined that these animals were "living symbols of the historic and pioneer spirit of the West." This recognition of the value of these animals simply existing and roaming free for their own sake formed the policy basis of the Act. Wild horses and burros were given co-equal status on public lands with livestock, wildlife, and other uses. Prior to 1971, the animals had no legal status and were subject to wholesale exploitation by meat and glue processing interests, with acquiescence and often the encouragement of state and local authorities.

The 1971 law required BLM and USFS to manage the herds only at the minimally necessary levels, the premise being that these animals should be left alone and interfered with only when they encroach upon other legitimate uses of the public lands. Criminal sanctions for capturing or harrassing [*sic*] these animals included imprisonment. In order to eliminate the profit motive, the sale of any captured horse or any commercial use of the animals' remains was prohibited. Most significantly for the HSUS, the Act mandated the humane treatment for captured animals. Old, lame, or diseased animals were permitted to be destroyed in the most humane manner possible. The adopted animals were also to be assured humane conditions. Capture and removal operations were to be done under federal supervision. Captured animals were placed with private individuals under adoption contracts whereby the federal government retained title to the animals and the adopter agreed to care for the animals properly. Adopted horses could be transferred only with government consent. This scheme was designed to prevent horses from being laundered through owners into slaughterhouses.

This Act seemed adequate to protect the animals. Unfortunately, BLM has favored livestock interests for decades and did not properly enforce the Act. Lawsuits against BLM were required to obtain minimal compliance. BLM alleged that there was continual overpopulation of the ranges by wild horses and argued for the annual removal of the horses. However, the population statistics cited by the agency have been shown to be inadequate and unreliable.

The adoption program was mismanaged by BLM. Captured horses were frequently corralled for long periods because BLM's recruitment of adopters was inefficient.

Prospective adopters sometimes waited for up to two years. BLM's enforcement of the humane clause of the adoption contract has also been lax. Horses have been abused both in the corrals and by adopters.

Congress accepted BLM's arguments against the horses and in 1978 passed legislation and strengthened BLM's authority to deal with the alleged overpopulation of the herds. BLM is now directed to remove any animals determined to be "excess" and dispose of the excess either by adoption or "humane and cost-efficient" destruction.

To dispose of more horses through adoption, an incentive was provided. After one year under adoption contracts, full ownership will be granted to the adopter. The horses then would no longer be protected federally.

The 1978 amendments limit to four, except under special written authorization, the number of animals any individual can adopt in one year, and require that BLM determine that the individual has properly cared for the animals during the one-year adopting period before title passes. Also, it remains unlawful to sell any horse or burro, or its remains, for processing into commercial products.

Finally, the 1978 amendments require BLM to maintain a current inventory of horses and burros on public lands and provide for a research study under the aegis of the National Academy of Sciences to supply needed, scientifically gathered information on the herds and their relation to the habitat. Congress intended this information to determine the extent of range overpopulation, and form the basis for more rational management of the herds in the future.

For further information contact:

Division of Range
Bureau of Land Management
Department of the Interior
Washington, D.C. 20240

Range Management
U.S. Forest Service
Department of Agriculture
Washington, D.C. 20013

THE MIGRATORY BIRD TREATY ACT (16 U.S.C. § 701 et seq.; passed 1918 and amended 1960 and 1969). This statute, administered by the Fish and Wildlife Service (Department of the Interior), protects various species of migratory birds by federal regulation from all forms of capture, harrassment [*sic*], or death, including sport hunting. The original Act was passed in 1918 to effectuate the treaty concluded in 1916 between the British Crown (on behalf of Canada) and the United States for the purposes of "saving from indiscriminate slaughter" and "insuring the preservation of" specific species of migratory birds. Treaty Conventions, Preamble, 39 Stat. 1702. Later, similar treaties with Mexico (1936) and with Japan (1972) were also given effect by the MBTA. The treaties essentially proclaimed that hunting of migratory game birds would be restricted to a three and one-half month period of each year, to occur between September 1 and March 10.

The heart of the MBTA consists of two sections: 16 U.S.C. § 703 is a sweeping *prohibition* of the killing, taking, hunting, capture, etc., of any migratory bird species included in the treaty conventions; 16 U.S.C. § 704 is a broad grant of discretion to the Secretary of the Interior to *allow* the killing, taking, hunting, capture, etc., of such migratory birds when and to the extent, if at all, such acts are compatible with the purposes and terms of the treaty conventions, and in so determining, the Secretary is explicitly charged by the Act to have "due regard to the zones of temperature and to the distribution, abundance, economic value, breeding habits, and times and lines of migratory flight" of migratory bird species.

The purpose of the MBTA is clearly to protect and ensure the preservation of *species* of migratory birds, as distinct from individual birds of even large numbers of birds within a species. This legally permits the hunting and slaughter of literally millions of individuals within a particular species of bird so long as the population of that species is not critically depressed.

For further information, contact:

Office of Migratory Bird Management
U.S. Fish and Wildlife Service
Department of the Interior
Washington, D.C. 20240

THE TWENTY-EIGHT HOUR LAW (45 U.S.C. § 71 et seq.; passed 1906). This statute was the first federal anti-cruelty law in the United States. The current law was enacted in 1906 and was a revision of a law passed in 1877.

The law applies to livestock in interstate transportation and prohibits railroads from confining livestock in boxcars for more than twenty-eight hours without unloading, resting, feeding, and watering the animals for at least five consecutive hours. Owners of a particular shipment, upon written request, may be granted an extension allowing a total of thirty-six hours for confinement without rest. Violators of this law are subject to fines of up to $500. The United States Department of Agriculture enforces this law.

For further information contact:

Secretary of Agriculture
Washington, D.C. 20250

THE ENDANGERED SPECIES ACT (7 U.S.C. § 136, 16 U.S.C. § 1531 et seq., P.L. 95–632; passed 1969, amended 1973 and 1978). The Endangered Species Act protects those species of plants and animals which are endangered or threatened with extinction over all or a significant portion of their habitats. The Act regulates the taking of species, restricts trade of such species and their by-products through a permit system, and, through regulations, protects species habitat from significant environmental modification or degradation. It also provides for the acquisition of habitat needed for the survival of a species and requires that all federal agencies avoid making adverse impacts which may threaten the survival of a species.

The type of restriction on the taking of or trade in a particular species and its by-products depends on whether it is listed as "threatened" or "endangered." Endangered species are closer to extinction than threatened species; therefore, endangered species have a higher degree of protection. Species are often listed as threatened if they are a likely candidate for endangered status because of trade or habitat encroachment pressure. Through the Endangered Species Act, international wildlife treaties are implemented. There are two important exemptions to the Endangered Species Act: (1) animals which are held in captivity prior to passage of the 1973 amendments; (2) Alaskan natives are allowed to hunt species if their hunting is primarily to supply subsistence needs. There are both civil and criminal penalties to punish violators of this law. The United States Department of the Interior, Fish and Wildlife Service, administers this law.

The Endangered Species Act also authorizes establishment of cooperative agreements and grants-in-aid to states with adequate conservation programs for endangered and threatened species.

The 1978 amendments significantly weakened the protective provisions, particularly for non-vertebrates. A cabinet level committee was established for the purpose of resolving conflicts between species and federal projects such as a dam. By a vote of 5 out of 7, the committee can order the extinction of a species in favor of a development project. The committee has been mandated to take economic data under consideration when deciding on an exemption application.

For further information, contact:

Director
U.S. Fish and Wildlife Service
Department of Interior
Washington, D.C. 20240

Some Common Questions About Animal Rights

(For Discussion with Children)

Why animal rights? Aren't they just dumb animals? How can dumb things have rights?

It is not necessary to be intelligent in order to have rights. Lots of people are dumb (i.e., unable to talk) or mentally handicapped, and little babies are dumb too. What is important here is the capacity to suffer, not the capacity to talk or reason. How about your own pet? A cat or dog can tell you what it wants, and quite often, how it feels, be it angry, playful, sulky, or tired.

So what's in it for me?

A better world; because when people respect the rights of animals they are more likely to respect each other's rights as well. Respecting animals' rights can therefore help improve society and help save nature from being destroyed.

Why can't we kill any animal that we want to since animals can kill each other if they want?

We have choices. They don't. Many animals have to kill others for food. For us this is rarely a survival necessity.

What about making animals suffer or die so that we can be healthy?

Some people say that if we don't use chimpanzees and other animals in cancer research, for example, we will never find a cure. Other people say that we should try to *prevent* cancers and that means cutting down on the pollution of our environment and improving our diets. Making monkeys and other animals suffer isn't the only way to a solution.

Doesn't the Bible say that God has given us the right to use animals for whatever purposes we might choose?

A lot of people interpret the statement in Genesis that God gave us dominion over the animals as his giving us permission to do whatever we like to them. But this means domination, doesn't it? Dominion should be interpreted as *careful stewardship*. There are many passages in the Bible that tell us to be kind to animals.

Does this mean that we should not eat meat?

If we can't go all the way and be vegetarians, we should at least try to go part way and eat less animals, and make sure that they have been humanely raised, transported, and slaughtered.

Chief Seattle's Letter to President Franklin Pierce

in response to the US government's proposal to purchase large tracts of land from the Indians and grant them reservations later

"How can you buy or sell the sky, the warmth of the land? The idea is strange to us.

"If we do not own the freshness of the air and the sparkle of the water, how can you buy them?

"Every part of the earth is sacred to my people. Every shining pine needle, every sandy shore, every mist in the dark woods, every clearing and humming insect is holy in the memory and experience of my people. The sap which courses through the trees carried the memories of the Red Man.

"The White Man's dead forgot the country of their birth when they go to walk among the stars. Our dead never forget this beautiful earth, for it is the mother of the Red Man. We are part of the earth, and it is part of us. The perfumed flowers are our sisters; the deer, the horse, the great eagle, these are our brothers. The rocky crests, the juices in the meadows, the body heat of the pony, and man—all belong to the same family.

"So, when the Great Chief in Washington sends word that

he wishes to buy our land, he asks much of us. The Great Chief sends word that he will reserve us a place so that we can live comfortably to ourselves. He will be our father, and we will be his children. So we will consider your offer to buy our land, but it will not be easy, for this land is sacred to us.

"This shining water that moves in the streams and rivers is not just water, but the blood of our ancestors. If we sell you land, you must remember that it is sacred, and you must teach your children that it is sacred, and that each ghostly reflection in the clear water of the lakes tells of events and memories in the life of my people. The water's murmur is the voice of my father's father.

"The rivers are our brothers, and they quench our thirst. The rivers carry our canoes, and feed our children. If we sell you our land, you must remember, and teach your children that the rivers are our brothers and yours, and you must henceforth give the rivers the kindness you would give any brother.

"We know that the White Man does not understand our ways. One portion of land is the same to him as the next, for he is a stranger who comes in the night, and takes from the land whatever he needs. The earth is not his brother, but his enemy, and when he has conquered it, he moves on. He leaves his father's graves behind, and he does not care. He kidnaps the earth from his children, and he does not care.

"His fathers' graves and his children's birthrights are forgotten. He treats his mother, the earth, and his brother, the sky, as things to be bought, plundered, sold like sheep or bright beads. His appetite will devour the earth, and leave behind only a desert.

"I do not know. Our ways are different from your ways. The sight of your cities pains the eyes of the Red Man, but perhaps it is because the Red Man is a savage and does not understand.

"There is no quiet place in the White Man's cities. No place to hear the unfurling of the leaves in spring or the rustle of the insects' wings. But perhaps it is because I am a savage and do not understand. The clatter seems only to insult the ears. What is there to life if a man cannot hear the lonely cry of the whipoorwill, or the arguments of the frogs around the pool at night? I am a Red Man, and do not understand. The Indian prefers the soft sound of the wind darting over the face of a pond, and the smell of the wind itself, cleansed by mid-day rain, or scented with the pinon pine.

"The air is precious to the Red Man, for all things share the same breath—the beast, the tree, the man, they all share the same breath. The white man does not seem to notice the air he breathes. Like a man dying for many days, he is numb to the stench. But if we sell you our land, you must remember that the air is precious to us, that the air shares its spirit with all the life it supports. The wind that gave our grandfather his first breath also received his last sigh. And if we sell you our land, you must keep it apart and sacred, as a place where even the White Man can go to taste the wind that is sweetened by the meadow's flowers.

"So we will consider your offer to buy our land. If we decide to accept, I will make one condition: the White Man must treat the beasts of the land as his brothers.

"I am a savage and do not understand any other way. I have seen a thousand rotting buffaloes on the prairie, left by the White Man who shot them from a passing train. I am a savage, and I do not understand how the smoking iron horse can be more important than the buffalo that we kill only to stay alive.

"What is man without the beasts? If all the beasts were gone man would die from a great loneliness of spirit. For whatever happens to the beasts, soon happens to man. All things are connected."